T0320660

SUPERCOMPUTER ARCHITECTURE

THE KLUWER INTERNATIONAL SERIES IN ENGINEERING AND COMPUTER SCIENCE

PARALLEL PROCESSING AND FIFTH GENERATION COMPUTING

Consulting Editor

Doug DeGroot

Other books in the series:

Parallel Execution of Logic Programs, John S. Conery. ISBN 0–89838–194–0.

Parallel Computation and Computers For Artificial Intelligence, Janusz S. Kowalik. ISBN 0–89838–227–0.

Memory Storage Patterns in Parallel Processing, Mary E. Mace. ISBN 0–89838–239–4.

Assignment Problems in Parallel and Distributed Computing, Shahid H. Bokhari. ISBN 0–89838–240–8.

SUPERCOMPUTER ARCHITECTURE

by

Paul B. Schneck
Supercomputing Research Center
Lanham, Maryland

KLUWER ACADEMIC PUBLISHERS
Boston/Dordrecht/Lancaster

Distributors for North America:
Kluwer Academic Publishers
101 Philip Drive
Assinippi Park
Norwell, Massachusetts 02061, USA

Distributors for the UK and Ireland:
Kluwer Academic Publishers
MTP Press Limited
Falcon House, Queen Square
Lancaster LA1 1RN, UNITED KINGDOM

Distributors for all other countries:
Kluwer Academic Publishers Group
Distribution Centre
Post Office Box 322
3300 AH Dordrecht, THE NETHERLANDS

Library of Congress Cataloging-in-Publication Data

Schneck, Paul B.
  Supercomputer architecture.

  (The Kluwer international series in
engineering and computer science ; SECS 31)
  Bibliography: p.
  Includes index.
  1. Supercomputers.   2. Computer architecture.
I. Title. II. Series.
QA76.5.S2725 1987   004.1'1   87–16942
ISBN 978-0-89838-238-9

To my wife,
for her inspiration
and
for her help.
Without her,
this book would not have been written.

Contents

List of Figures   ix

List of Tables   xi

Preface   xiii

1	Introduction	1
2	The IBM 7030 Stretch	7
3	The CDC 6600	35
4	The IBM 360–91	53
5	The CDC STAR-100	99
6	The ILLIAC IV	119
7	The CRAY-1	135
8	The CYBER 205	155
9	The Massively Parallel Processor	165
	References and Bibliography	189
	Index	197

FIGURES

2.1	The Stretch	9
2.2	Index Register Format	10
2.3	Standard instruction format	12
2.4	Specialized Instruction Formats	13
2.5	Central processing unit	22
2.6	Instruction Control Unit	24
2.7	Instruction Look-ahead Registers	26
2.8	Serial Arithmetic Unit	30
2.9	Parallel Arithmetic Unit	33
3.1	The CDC 6600	36
3.2	Instruction Formats	38
3.3	Core Memory Timing	44
3.4	Magnetic Core Wiring	45
3.5	The Stunt Box	46
3.6	The Instruction Stack	49
4.1	Register to register instruction format	57
4.2	Register to storage instruction format	58
4.3	Storage to storage instruction format	58
4.4	Storage-immediate instruction format	59
4.5	Instruction buffer array	65
4.6	Instruction issue register	68
4.7	Fixed-point execution unit	71
4.8	Floating-point execution unit	73
4.9	The common data bus	81
4.10	The floating-point adder	84
4.11	The floating-point multiplier	88
4.12	The floating-point divider	92

4.13	The main storage control element	95
5.1	The STAR 100 Central Processor	101
5.2	Storage Access Control	103
5.3	The Stream Unit	106
5.4	Instruction Stack	107
5.5	Pipeline 1	109
5.6	Pipeline 2	109
5.7	Instruction Format	111
6.1	Control unit block diagram	121
6.2	Control unit registers	123
6.3	Processing unit	125
6.4	Processing element	126
6.5	Instruction formats	131
7.1	The Cray processor	137
7.2	Instruction Formats	141
7.3	Multiply pyramid	143
7.4	Instruction processing mechanism	147
7.5	Chaining data flow	151
7.6	Non-chain timing	152
7.7	Chaining	153
8.1	The CYBER 205	156
8.2	Scalar processor	158
8.3	Vector processor	161
8.4	Floating-point pipeline	162
8.5	Floating-point add unit	162
8.6	Floating-point multiply/divide unit	163
9.1	Massively parallel processor	167
9.2	Array unit	168
9.3	Processor element	170
9.4	Interconnection topologies	172
9.5	Corner bit selection	174
9.6	Array control unit	177
9.7	Processor element control unit	179
9.8	Staging buffer	184

TABLES

1.1	Rate of Increase of Computer Speed	3
2.1	Logical operation specification	17
2.2	Index increment	20
2.3	Instruction-Unit Counter Control	27
2.4	Transfer-Bus Counter Control	28
2.5	Arithmetic-Bus Counter Control	28
2.6	Store-Check Counter Control	29
4.1	Instruction fetch control	64
4.2	Floating-point instruction characteristics	74
5.1	Floating-Point Speeds	100
7.1	Function Unit Timing	142

PREFACE

Supercomputers are the largest and fastest computers available at any point in time. The term was used for the first time in the *New York World*, March 1920, to describe "new statistical machines with the mental power of 100 skilled mathematicians in solving even highly complex algebraic problems." Invented by Mendenhall and Warren, these machines were used at Columbia University's Statistical Bureau.

Recently, supercomputers have been used primarily to solve large-scale problems in science and engineering. Solutions of systems of partial differential equations, such as those found in nuclear physics, meteorology, and computational fluid dynamics, account for the majority of supercomputer use today.

The early computers, such as EDVAC, SSEC, 701, and UNIVAC, demonstrated the feasibility of building fast electronic computing machines which could become commercial products. The next generation of computers focused on attaining the highest possible computational speeds. This book discusses the architectural approaches used to yield significantly higher computing speeds while preserving the conventional, von Neumann, machine organization (Chapters 2–4). Subsequent improvements depended on developing a new generation of computers employing a new model of computation: single-instruction multiple-data (SIMD) processors (Chapters 5–7). Later machines refined SIMD architecture and technology (Chapters 8-9).

SUPERCOMPUTER ARCHITECTURE

CHAPTER 1

INTRODUCTION

THREE ERAS OF SUPERCOMPUTERS

Supercomputers -- the largest and fastest computers available at any point in time -- have been the products of complex interplay among technological, architectural, and algorithmic developments. The history of supercomputers depicts the dominance of each of these developments at particular times and divides naturally into three eras: (a) technology, (b) architecture, and (c) algorithms.

The Technology Era (1945 to 1970) was characterized by the rapid introduction of new families of circuit devices. The earliest computers (in today's parlance, mere calculating machines), produced in the mid-1940s, were electromechanical devices comprised of relays acting as logic gates. Soon thereafter, vacuum tubes replaced relays as logical devices. Where relays operated in milliseconds, vacuum tubes required only microseconds. Computing speeds increased by orders of magnitude, allowing the solution of problems previously out of reach.

By the end of the 1950s, transistors (*solid state* devices) replaced vacuum tubes. Those pea-sized devices, which consumed little power and generated little heat, were faster and far more reliable than their predecessors. The combination of high reliability and low power of solid-state devices led to the development of complex processors containing more circuits than ever before possible. The IBM 7030, CDC 6600, and IBM 360 model 91 are examples of such machines.

The IBM 360 series, introduced in 1964, epitomized opportunities made possible by densely packed circuits. Built with internally developed hybrid circuits, called solid logic technology (SLT) by IBM, the System/360 has 143 instructions. These instructions are divided into groups specialized for floating-point arithmetic, fixed-point arithmetic, logical operations, character operations, and operating system processing. The IBM 360 architecture remains dominant today.

Although integrated circuits appeared in the 1970s, they have not yet had a profound impact on supercomputer development. Current supercomputers are built of circuits containing gates numbered from a few to a few hundred. Circuits in the Cray 1 are built of chips containing only two logic gates. The Cray XMP uses chips with 16 logic gates. The ETA 10, a multiprocessor currently in development and based on the Cyber 205, features gate arrays of 20,000 gates and is planned to be an order of magnitude faster than the Cyber 205.

The pace of technological improvement has not been fast enough to satisfy the needs of the user community. Despite the introduction of new technologies, the increase of computer speeds has continued to decrease. Table 1.1, prepared by Dale Henderson of Los Alamos National Laboratory, clearly depicts the slowing down of the rate of increase in computer speed. As component speeds increase, the delays caused by transmission of electricity through passive components becomes a limiting factor. Thus, speed improvements due to technology are more difficult to achieve, and innovative architectural approaches are required to attain increased performance.

The "easy" things are done first -- and so it was with architecture. The Architecture Era began with the inclusion of such features as instruction/execution overlap, memory cache, and execution pipelines. The most recent architectural advances have been more challenging, resulting in the current vector supercomputers and plans for a number of (experimental) parallel machines.

Midpoint	Years to double
1952	1.45
1962	2.06
1972	2.93
1982	4.17

Table 1.1 Rate of Increase of Computer Speed

During the coming Algorithms Era, emphasis will be placed on mathematics and computer science techniques aimed at discovering concurrence within a problem and exploiting an architecture to achieve concurrent execution.

Architectural evolution

A variety of architectural developments were used to increase computer speed beyond that which technology could offer. The evolution of these developments is recorded in the machines described below.

The IBM 7030 was designed to provide a speed increase of 2 orders of magnitude beyond existing machines. Technology was to provide a factor of 10, and architecture was to provide another factor of 10. The instruction set was large and specialized. Instructions were included whenever they were expected to provide a speed advantage. An instruction look-ahead unit overlapped processing of several instructions. Elaborate optimizations were employed to reduce the apparent access time of the 2 microsecond core memory. Data were prefetched, combined, or forwarded to reduce the number of storage accesses. Registers were reserved, a technique that would reach fruition as the common data bus of the IBM 360 model 91.

The CDC 6600 introduced interleaved memory, multiple functional (execution) units, and an extensive instruction scheduling mechanism, the scoreboard. With three sets of registers, floating-point, fixed-point, and index, the CDC 6600's basic architecture is found again in the CDC 7600, Cray 1, Cray XMP, and Cray 2.

The IBM 360 model 91 incorporated the architectural features found most advantageous on the IBM 7030. Instruction overlap and instruction look-ahead were extended to a separate, autonomous unit. Floating-point arithmetic was carried out by an autonomous unit. The common data bus, an extension of the reservation scheme of the IBM 7030, decoupled instruction processing from storage access time. Today, a variant of the common data bus is used on the Cray 1 and its successor machines.

The CDC STAR-100 introduced *vector processing*. The STAR provided a very high stream rate (10^8 instructions per second) for data existing as a sequence (vector), although a long period of time, termed *latency*, was required until the first result appeared. Subsequent results appeared at a rate of 10^8 per second. The STAR used the vector arithmetic unit to process all data, including scalar data where each instruction was delayed by the vector unit latency. As Amdahl's law [AMD67] indicates, the performance of such a system is dominated by the time required to perform the slowest operations.

The ILLIAC IV consisted of 64 separately-functioning, but commonly directed, processing elements. The ILLIAC IV provided an effective speed of up to 64 times the speed of a single processor. The challenge was in obtaining that speed. Without significant work, many programs utilized only a single processor while others remained idle, achieving no speed increase at all. The advantages of the ILLIAC IV's parallel architecture remain. First, there are economies of scale in the design and manufacture of 64 identical processing elements. Additionally, the investment in a control unit may be amortized over multiple processing elements. As an experimental device, the ILLIAC IV demonstrated that it was possible to achieve significant speed increases by using 64 processors in tandem. However, the ILLIAC IV was not easy to use, or in today's terms "user friendly", and until recently, there have been no commercial machines built with its parallel architecture.

The Cray 1 vector processing system architecture is similar to that of the CDC 6600. It may be useful to envision the Cray 1 as a CDC 6600 with A, B, and X registers which are each 64 elements *deep*. The Cray 1 differs from the STAR in providing registers for arithmetic vector operations. In fact, arithmetic operations may be performed only on quantities already in registers. Separate fetch and store instructions are provided to move data between the registers and storage. The data flow among registers and functional unit exploits features of the IBM 360 model 91's common data bus. *Chaining*, the ability to perform two operations on a pair of operands while in transit, is similar to *data chaining* in the IBM 7030 and in the IBM 360 model 91.

The CDC CYBER 205 is an improved version of the STAR. Separate arithmetic units are provided for vector and scalar instructions. Scalar instructions no longer suffer a long latency time. Both scalar and vector instructions may be performed concurrently.

The Massively Parallel Processor (MPP) is a direct descendant of the ILLIAC IV. Although containing 16,384 processors instead of 64, and using a 1-bit arithmetic element instead of a 64-bit floating-point unit, the MPP is otherwise similar to the ILLIAC IV. Each processor is connected to its 4 nearest neighbors, and can be directed to skip a sequence of instructions while other processors execute it. Although providing a large increase in speed, it is a challenge to structure data to exploit the potential speed of the Massively Parallel Processor, and an even greater challenge to program applications to run efficiently.

The chapters following detail the architectural advances of each of these machines.

CHAPTER 2

THE IBM 7030: STRETCH

PERSPECTIVE

In 1956 the Atomic Energy Commission contracted with IBM to build a computer system, the IBM 7030, for the Los Alamos Scientific Laboratory. This system was to be 100 times faster than existing machines. The machine was to be built using the newly available solid state components (transistors, diodes, magnetic cores) instead of vacuum tubes. Use of semiconductors would permit higher reliability and higher speed. The speed of a floating-point addition was planned to be less than 1 microsecond, and the 8,192 word memory units were to have a speed of 2 microseconds.

The Atomic Energy Commission's approach to acquiring computers is notable. Ambitious, sometimes unattainable, goals were set for the Los Alamos machine. These goals caused IBM to *stretch* the state of the art, giving the IBM 7030 its popular name [BUC62, BLO59]. Upon completion, Stretch fell short of the stated goals. Nonetheless, it was accepted by the government because it was the fastest machine available. The AEC's approach continued for over two decades and was an important force in shaping the development of supercomputers.

ARCHITECTURE

At the inception of the project to build Stretch, the model 704 was IBM's fastest computer. Stretch resembled the model 704, with augmentations and improvements based upon experience and new technology. At the time Stretch was designed, high level languages were not yet a dominant force in programming. Fortran was under development; assembly languages were widely used for large-scale programming tasks; and machine-language debugging, even machine-language programming, was common.

Stretch is composed of five independent elements (Figure 2.1) operating concurrently:

1. The central processing unit interprets instructions and performs arithmetic and logical operations.

2. The memory units hold program instructions and data. Up to 16 memory units can be attached to a system. Each magnetic-core memory unit contains 16,384 words of 64 bits, plus eight bits for error detection and correction. The cycle time of the memory is 2 microseconds.

3. The memory bus unit takes requests to fetch or store data in the memory from the exchange, the disk synchronizer unit, and the central processor.

4. The disk synchronizer unit and associated high speed disk drives provide high-capacity and high-speed disk storage capability for temporary storage of data during program execution.

5. The exchange is comprised of eight input-output channels which operate independently, reading data from, or writing data to, attached peripheral devices such as magnetic tapes, disks, card readers, line printers, and consoles.

Registers

Stretch contains a large number of   registers, providing specialized functions and capabilities. Unless indicated, a register occupies an entire 64-bit data word. Some registers (or register fields) are read-only; others may be set by storing a value. The instruction counter is the only register not assigned a memory location. In later systems, registers were grouped together according to function, allowing a set of registers to be modified at one time.. The program status word (PSW) of the IBM 360 is an example.

Instruction Counter. The 18-bit instruction counter (IC) indicates the address of the next instruction. It is advanced or modified during instruction execution. At the completion of an instruction, the instruction indicated by the IC is executed.

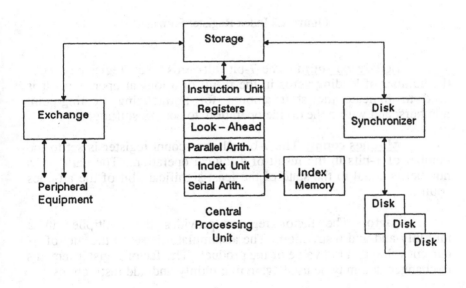

Figure 2.1 The Stretch

Accumulator. The accumulator register occupies two words of storage, holding the double-length (128-bit) result of arithmetic operations. Each 64-bit word is individually addressable.

Sign-byte. The 8-bit sign-byte register holds two 4-bit sign and flag fields for the high-order and low-order accumulator words.

Index. The sixteen index registers, X_0-X_{15}, are each comprised of four fields: (a) the *value* field, which when added to the address specified within an instruction, forms the effective address; (b) the *count* field, which is decremented each time the index is used; (c) the *refill* address, which specifies the storage location from which the index will be refilled when the count field reaches zero; and (d) the *chain and control bits* field, which indicates whether an index register is to be refilled when the count reaches zero (Figure 2.2).

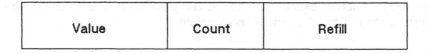

Figure 2.2 Index Register Format

Left-zeros count. The 7-bit left-zeros count register is set to the number of leading zeros in the result of a logical operation. It is used to indicate the shift amount for normalizing floating-point numbers, and within the divide operation, to control shifting.

All-ones count. The 7-bit all-ones count register is set to the number of 1-bits in the result of a logical operation. The parity of a number is equal to the state of the least-significant bit of the all-ones count.

Factor. The factor register provides the multiplier in a multiply-and-add instruction. The accumulator is set to the sum of its current value and the value of the product. The factor register remains unchanged and may be used again in multiply-and-add instructions.

Remainder. The remainder register receives the signed remainder of a divide instruction.

Transit. The transit register holds a subroutine parameter and is used as a mechanism for extending the instruction set. In current machines, the functions of the transit register are included with those of the general-purpose registers.

Mask. The mask register controls the action taken when an interrupt condition occurs. If the corresponding bit of the mask register is a 1-bit, the interrupt is taken; if it is a 0-bit, the interrupt is not taken. Twenty-eight mask bits may be set or reset under program control; sixteen are permanently 0-bits, and twenty are permanently 1-bits. The program may test for pending interrupts which have been disallowed by a 0-bit in the mask register.

Indicator. The indicator register records whether interrupt conditions have occurred and are pending. If the corresponding bit of the mask register is set (1-bit), the interrupt is allowed and the indicator bit is cleared. If the corresponding bit of the mask register is reset (0-bit), the interrupt remains pending until tested or allowed.

Zero. The zero register supplies the constant zero whenever it is referenced. It retains the value zero even after use as a result location.

Interval timer. The 19-bit interval timer is decremented once per millisecond. It may be set by the program and generates an interrupt condition when it reaches zero.

Clock. The 36-bit clock is incremented once per millisecond. It may not be altered by the program and provides a reference value indicating the length of time a program has run.

Address-boundary. The upper-address boundary register and lower-address boundary register are each 18-bits long and specify the addressing limits of a protected area. Any reference outside the protected area is disallowed, and a program interruption is generated. The use of the boundary registers permits checking address references concurrently with execution.

Boundary-control. The setting of the 1-bit boundary-control register determines whether the address-boundary registers specify the area in which references are allowed or whether they specify the area in which references are disallowed.

Instruction Format

The instruction set of Stretch is organized into families, with modifier bits distinguishing instruction operation. Instructions are either full words (64-bits) or half words (32-bits), as shown in Figure

2.3.   Typically, full-word instructions are used with operations involving (a) two operands in storage or (b) a variable-field-length operand requiring additional description (e.g. length and byte size). These instructions generally specify an operation and either the storage addresses of its two operands or the beginning address and modifiers of its explicit operand.   Half-word instructions typically are used with operations involving word-oriented data (e.g. fixed-point and floating-point arithmetic).   They generally specify an operation and the storage address of its second operand.   The first operand is an implied register (e.g. the accumulator).

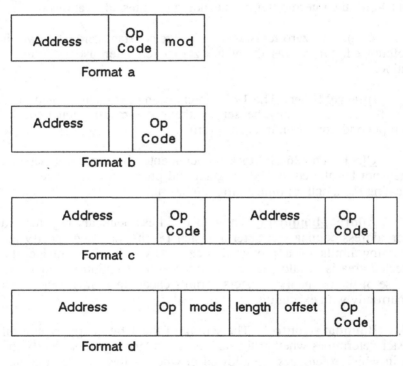

Format a

Format b

Format c

Format d

Figure 2.3 Standard instruction format

To achieve the speed goal set for Stretch, specialized instructions were added whenever it was deemed they would be frequently utilized.   Unique instruction formats were introduced to accommodate these specialized instructions (Figure 2.4).   Modifier fields in each instruction further expanded the number of instructions available to the programmer to a total of 735.

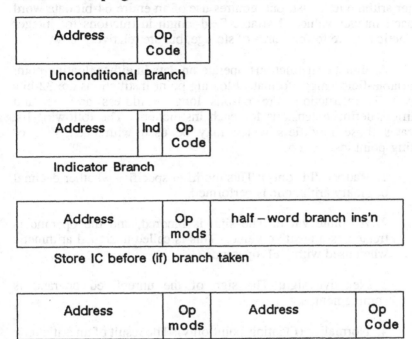

Figure 2.4 Specialized Instruction Formats

Instructions

Stretch has five major families of instructions: (a) arithmetic, (b) logical and data transmission, (c) index, (d) branch, and (e) input and output. Instructions from the first four families directly influence the design and implementation of the central processor and are defined below.

Arithmetic Instructions. Stretch performs arithmetic in two basic modes: (a) variable-field-length (VFL) and (b) floating-point. Integer arithmetic is available either by using unnormalized floating-point arithmetic operations or by using variable-field-length operations. The use of unnormalized floating-point operations for integer arithmetic is fast, but requires use of an entire 64-bit data word for each integer value. Variable-field-length instructions for integer arithmetic require fewer words of storage, but are relatively slow.

Arithmetic instructions operate on data in either floating-point or variable-field-length format. Floating point instructions are 32-bits long; VFL instructions are 64-bits long. Address and operand modifiers define extensions for each instruction. The following list indicates those modifiers which may be used with each VFL or floating-point instruction.

1. Radix (VFL only): This modifier specifies whether decimal or binary arithmetic is performed.

2. Absolute value: The sign is ignored, and the operand is treated as a positive value. This is called unsigned arithmetic when used with VFL operands.

3. Negative sign: The sign of the unreplaced operand is complemented.

4. Normalize (Floating-point only): The result of an arithmetic operation is normalized.

5. Immediate address: The effective address generated after indexing is used as the operand.

6. Progressive indexing: The index value is used as the effective address, and subsequently is increased (decreased) by a specified value. Use of this modifier enables the index to be altered concurrently with execution of the arithmetic instruction, and eliminates the need for a separate instruction to modify the index register.

The following operations are available in both floating-point and VFL instruction modes (Parentheses indicate an additional instruction definition.):

1. Add: Set the accumulator to the sum of the accumulator and the storage operand. Subtraction is indicated by a modifier bit which complements the sign bit of the storage operand.

2. Add to memory: Set the storage operand to the sum of the accumulator and the storage operand. Subtraction is indicated by a modifier bit which complements the sign bit of the storage operand.

3. Add to magnitude: Set the accumulator to the sum of the storage operand and the magnitude of the accumulator. The accumulator is set to zero if its sign differs from that of the sum.

4. Add magnitude to memory: Set the storage operand to the sum of the magnitude of the accumulator and the storage operand. The storage operand is set to zero if its sign differs from that of the sum.

5. Multiply: Set the accumulator to the product of the accumulator and the storage operand. When decimal mode is specified, the operation is implemented by a subroutine.

6. Multiply and add: Set the accumulator to the sum of the accumulator and the product of the factor-register and the storage operand.

7. Divide: Set the accumulator to the quotient of the accumulator divided by the storage operand. In VFL mode, set the remainder register to the remainder after division.

8. Compare (magnitude): The indicator register is set to reflect the result of the comparison between the (magnitude of the) accumulator and the storage operand.

9. Compare (magnitude) for range: This instruction follows the compare (magnitude) instruction. The indicator register is set to reflect whether the (magnitude of the) accumulator falls below, within, or above the range defined by the two storage operands of this instruction and its predecessor.

10. Load (with flag): The accumulator (and flag bits) is (are) set to the value of the storage operand.

11. Load factor: The factor register is set to the value of the storage operand.

12. Store: The storage operand is set to the value of the accumulator, including the flag bits.

13. Store rounded: The storage operand is set to the rounded value of the accumulator.

The following operations are among those available only in floating-point instruction mode:

1. Add double: This operation is similar to add, with the accumulator supplying a 96-bit fraction.

2. Add double to magnitude: This operation is similar to add-to-magnitude, with the accumulator supplying a 96-bit fraction.

3. Multiply double: This operation is similar to multiply, with the accumulator supplying a 96-bit fraction.

4. Divide double: This operation is similar to divide, with the accumulator supplying a 96-bit fraction for the dividend. A single length quotient and remainder are placed in the accumulator and remainder register.

5. Reciprocal divide: Set the accumulator to the quotient of the storage operand divided by the accumulator.

6. Store root: The storage operand value is set to the square root of the accumulator.

The following operations are among those available only in VFL instruction mode:

1. Increment memory: The storage operand value is replaced by its original value plus one.

2. Compare if equal: The compare is performed only if the equal-indicator is set and is used to compare two VFL operands.

Logical and Data Transmission Instructions. There are three logical and two data transmission instructions. The logical instructions calculate any of the sixteen boolean functions of two operands. The data transmission instructions move operands between areas of storage. Both immediate addressing and progressive indexing are available for logical instructions. However, only immediate addressing is available for the count field of the data transmission instructions. If immediate addressing is not specified, the count field is obtained from an index register. A modifier bit indicates whether the operand field of a data transmission instruction is stored in ascending or descending storage locations.

A logical operation is chosen by specifying its output function in a 4-bit field, b_0, b_1, b_2, b_3, of the instruction modifier. In Table 2.1 below, a is an accumulator bit, and s is the corresponding bit of the storage operand.

a	s	b
0	0	b_0
0	1	b_1
1	0	b_2
1	1	b_3

Table 2.1 Logical operation specification

The logical instructions are:

1. Connect: Set the accumulator to the result of the specified logical operation of the accumulator and the storage operand. Set the left-zeros count register and the all-ones count register to reflect the result.

2. Connect to memory: Set the storage operand value to the result of the specified logical operation of the accumulator and the storage operand. Set the left-zeros count register and the all-ones count register to reflect the result.

3. Connect for test: Set the left-zeros count register and the all-ones count register to reflect the result of the specified logical operation of the accumulator and the storage operand. The accumulator and the storage operand remain unchanged.

The data transmission instructions are:

1. Transmit: The contents of the first area in storage replace the contents of the second area in storage.

2. Swap: The contents of any two areas of storage are exchanged.

Index instructions. Stretch has a large set of index register instructions. Any one of the value, count, or refill fields of an index register may be loaded. Further, most instructions also may be specified with an immediate operand, indicated by I. The immediate operand is itself used as a value, instead of as a storage address which points to a value. In the list below, V, C, and R stand for value, count, and refill field, respectively. Wherever an add operation is shown, a subtract operation also may be performed.

1. Load index: The index register is set to the value of the storage operand.

2. Store index: The storage operand is set to the value of the index register.

3. Load (V/C/R)(I): The specified field of the index register is set to the value of the operand. The operand is fetched from storage or, if immediate mode is specified, it is fetched from the instruction.

4. Store (V/C/R): The value of the specified field of the index register is stored in the corresponding field of the storage operand.

5. Store value in address: The value field of the index register is stored in the address field of the storage operand.

6. Add to (V/V,C/V,C,R)(I): The storage or immediate field operand is added to the value field of the index register. If

count is specified, the count field is decremented. If *refill* is also specified, the index register is loaded from the word specified by the refill address when the count reaches zero.

7. Compare (V/C)(I): The storage or immediate field operand is compared with the value or count field, and the index-comparison indicators are set.

8. Load value effective: An instruction is fetched from the effective address computed. If the instruction fetched is itself a *load value effective* instruction, the operation recurs. If not, the value field of the index register is set to the effective address of the fetched instruction.

9. Load value with sum: The value field of the index register is set to the sum of the value fields of those index registers indicated by a 1-bit in the instruction address field.

10. Rename: The index register is stored in the address specified by the refill field of X_0. The instruction's effective address is then placed in the refill field of X_0. Finally, the index register is loaded from that address.

Branch instructions. There are three classes of branch instructions: (a) bit test or indicator test, (b) index, and (c) unconditional. If a *store instruction counter if* instruction immediately precedes a successful branch, the contents of the instruction counter are stored at the specified address. This mechanism saves the return address of a subroutine call.

Bit test or indicator test branch instructions. Two modifier conditions, *on-off* and *zero*, are available both for bit tests and indicator tests. An *invert* modifier is available for the bit tests. A bit or indicator test succeeds (i.e. the branch is taken) when the bit or indicator tested, *t*, is the same as the *on-off* modifier. That is, when

t .eq. *on-off* ,

is true. The bit or indicator tested is reset if the *zero* modifier is set. That is,

$t = t$ .and. *~zero* .

After the *zero* modifier functions, the tested bit is inverted if the *invert* modifier is set. That is,

$$t = t \text{ .xor. } invert \text{ .}$$

The bit test and indicator test branch instructions are listed below:

1. Branch on bit: This instruction addresses a bit and branches if the test meets the condition specified by the *on-off* modifier.

2. Branch on indicator: This instruction addresses an indicator and branches if the test meets the condition specified by the *on-off* modifier.

Index branch instructions. Index branches interpret the *on-off* modifier in the context of the count field: (a) when *on-off* is 1, branch if the count goes to zero; (b) when *on-off* is 0, branch if the count does not go to zero. As shown in Table 2.2, a second modifier, *advance*, defines the quantity added to the value field.

advance	quantity
0	0
1	1/2
2	1
3	-1

Table 2.2 Index increment

The index branch instructions are listed below:

1. Count and branch: Increment the value field; decrement the count field; and branch if the count goes to zero.

2. Count, branch, and refill: This instruction is similar to count and branch, but when the count goes to zero, the index register is refilled.

Unconditional branch instructions. Three of the six unconditional branch instructions control the state of the interrupt system.   The *wait-bit*, which controls multiprogramming and multitasking on the IBM 360, is introduced in the Stretch.   The unconditional branch instructions are:

1. Branch: The instruction counter is set to the effective address.

2. No operation: The instruction counter is incremented normally.

3. Branch relative: The instruction counter is set to the sum of the instruction counter and the effective address.

4. Branch disabled: The interrupt system is disabled, and then the branch is taken.

5. Branch enabled: The interrupt system is enabled, and then the branch is taken.

6. Branch enabled and wait: The interrupt system is enabled, and no instructions are processed until an interrupt occurs.

IMPLEMENTATION PHILOSOPHY

The performance goal of the Stretch was to attain a speed of 100 times that of the IBM 704.   High-speed transistor circuitry provided a factor of ten, and new core-memory units provided a factor of only six.   To achieve the ambitious speed goal, a change in processor organization, coupled with an emphasis on the design of the instruction set, was necessary.   This increased concurrency and minimized delays due to the relatively slow memory units.

The instruction set was designed to be complete, yet systematic.   A small number of distinct instructions, expandable through modifiers, was provided.   Specialized instructions were defined for frequently occurring tasks that were implemented economically within the hardware facilities.   The resulting mix of general and specialized instructions allowed easy construction of compilers, while furnishing opportunities for programming experts.

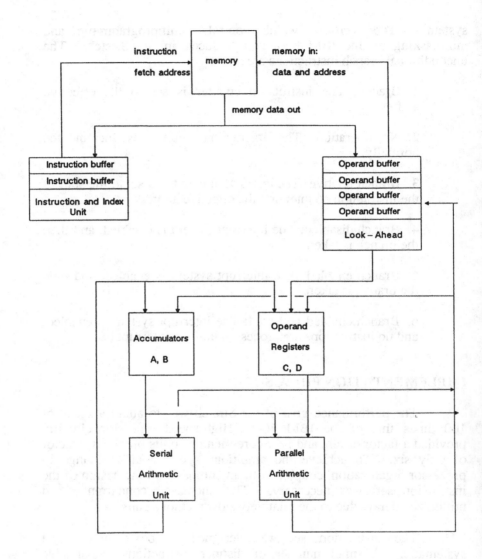

Figure 2.5 Central processing unit

THE CENTRAL PROCESSING UNIT

The central processing unit (CPU) is highly concurrent, processing up to four instructions at one time. Prior computers processed instructions sequentially. They fetched an instruction; decoded it; generated a memory address; fetched its operand; and performed the indicated operation. Stretch processes several instructions concurrently, in a pipelined mode. It can fetch two words containing up to four instructions; decode two instructions; fetch four operands; and execute instructions as operands arrive, all at one time. Interlocks ensure that results are independent of the order of operations and are the same as those that would be obtained by sequential instruction execution.

The central processing unit consists of four major components: (a) instruction control unit, (b) instruction look-ahead unit, (c) serial arithmetic unit, and (d) parallel arithmetic unit. These units (Figure 2.5) represent a radical departure in computer architecture, increasing the speed of Stretch beyond that which was available from technology.

Instruction Control Unit

The instruction control unit (ICU) fetches, decodes, and indexes instructions [BLO60]. Six instructions may be processed at once in the ICU (Figure 2.6). Up to four instructions (two 64-bit words) may be fetched at the same time as two previously fetched instructions are decoded and indexed. Instruction words fetched from memory are held in two instruction registers until the ICU removes them for processing.

The ICU executes branch and index instructions. Other instructions are sent to the instruction look-ahead unit after they have been partially decoded and operand fetches initiated.

The ICU deals with both unconditional and conditional branch instructions. Unconditional branch instructions are executed immediately by placing the branch address in the instruction counter. Conditional branches are executed immediately only if the test result is available. If not, the branch is forwarded for later execution, and instruction processing continues on the assumption that the branch will not be taken. If the assumption was incorrect and a branch later proves to be successful, then the ICU recovers by cancelling those instructions fetched after the branch and by beginning a new instruction sequence· at the branch address.

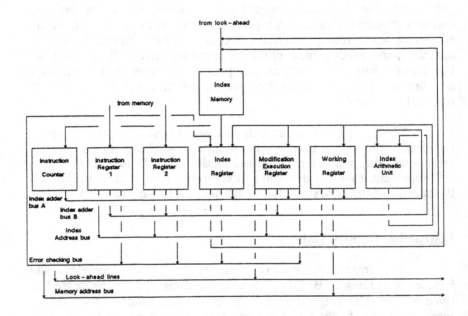

Figure 2.6 Instruction Control Unit

Index instructions are executed in the ICU. Although the sixteen index registers have memory addresses, they are implemented within the ICU to minimize transmission delays. A special high-speed memory unit is provided for the index registers. Most index operations need to read the index registers, and do not need to modify them. The index register memory unit is constructed with multiaperture magnetic cores, having a nondestructive read cycle, not requiring a restore cycle, and yielding a short read-access time. A small penalty results when an index register is modified, and a write cycle is required. This has little impact, as index register modifications usually occur in parallel with other instruction processing activities within the instruction control unit.

The ICU forwards instructions, along with data tags and the current value of the instruction counter, to the instruction look-ahead unit. The data tags and instruction counter are used to preserve the ordering of instructions and data.

Instruction Look-ahead Unit

The instruction look-ahead unit (ILU) uses parallelism to hide latency. The bandwidth of four 2 microsecond memory units yields an average access time of .5 microseconds per data word. This transfer rate is sufficiently high to sustain the parallel arithmetic unit. However, memory references do not occur with complete regularity, resulting in delays due to latency when fetching random data and in delays due to occasional memory-busy status. To minimize delays, the ILU processes a number of instructions simultaneously: (a) It holds data which arrive from memory in advance of instruction execution, and (b) it holds instructions until their data are available.

Only after data are received by the instruction look-ahead unit, are operations sent to the arithmetic units. System design is greatly simplified by separating instruction execution from the data access mechanism. The arithmetic units are not complicated with issues concerning availability of data. More importantly, since there is only one data access mechanism in the system, improvements are highly leveraged and substantial effort is invested in optimization.

The ILU has four levels of look-ahead. After preliminary decoding, the ICU places an instruction along with the data tags and the current value of the instruction counter (the next instruction location) into one of the levels of look-ahead (Figure 2.7). Each level of look-ahead also contains an operand field and a 15-bit indicator field.

The uses of the indicator bits associated with each instruction are evident from their names: (a) address invalid, (b) data fetch, (c) data store, (d) index count zero, (e) index equal, (f) index flag, (g) index high, (h) index low, (i) index value greater than zero, (j) index value less than zero, (k) index value zero, (l) instruction fetch, (m) instruction reject, (n) machine check, and (o) operation code invalid. At the conclusion of an instruction, the ILU transfers the indicator bits to the indicator register. The tags indicate the following conditions or status:

1. The level at which forwarding can occur;

2. A valid instruction counter which may be used if an interrupt occurs;

3. A register, not memory as the operand source;

4. A checked operand (e.g. parity);

5. A full operand field;

6. An operation intended for use by the look-ahead unit;

7. The need to force a null operation; and

8. The VFL operand spanning a word boundary.

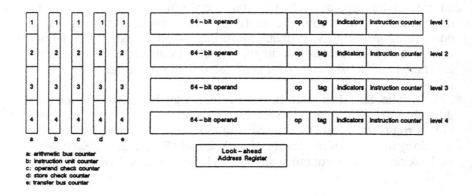

a: arithmetic bus counter
b: instruction unit counter
c: operand check counter
d: store check counter
e: transfer bus counter

Figure 2.7 Instruction Look-ahead Registers

Forwarding and *combining*, which appear later in the IBM 360 model 91, are used to avoid multiple references to one storage location. The data address of a store instruction is placed in the *look-ahead address register* (Fig. 2.7). If no store instructions are present in the

ILU, the address of the most recent load instruction is maintained in the look-ahead address register. The address of data required by an instruction is compared with the look-ahead address register. A match results in avoidance of a memory fetch and reuse of the prior instruction's data.

The ILU is comprised of five autonomous processes which prepare instructions for execution:

1. Instruction-unit counter control (Table 2.3);

2. Operand-check counter control (ensures that data are correct before allowing instruction processing to proceed);

3. Transfer-bus counter control (Table 2.4);

4. Arithmetic-bus counter control (Table 2.5); and

5. Store-check counter control (Table 2.6).

Decision	No, next decision
01 Store required?	06
02 Is a store operation in process?	04
03 GOTO	02
04 Hold address for forwarding	05
05 GOTO	14
06 Fetch required?	14
07 Is fetch address same as forwarding address?	11
08 Cancel fetch request	09
09 Forward data	10
10 GOTO	14
11 Does forwarding register contain a store address?	13
12 GOTO	14
13 Hold address for combining	14
14 Does instruction-unit counter=store-unit counter	16
15 GOTO (cannot get ahead of store)	14
16 Advance instruction-unit counter	17
17 GOTO	01

Table 2.3 Instruction-Unit Counter Control

Decision	No, next decision
01 Is instruction a floating-point fetch?	07
02 Send operation code and operand to arithmetic unit	03
03 Has arithmetic unit accepted?	03
04 Does transfer-bus counter=operand-check counter?	06
05 GOTO	04
06 Advance transfer-bus counter	01
07 Is instruction a floating-point store?	06
08 Send operation code to arithmetic unit	09
09 GOTO	03

Table 2.4 Transfer-Bus Counter Control

Decision	No, next decision
01 Is instruction a floating-point fetch/store?	06
02 Transmit indicators to indicator register	03
03 Is instruction a store?	06
04 Is store data available?	04
05 Get data from arithmetic unit	06
06 Does arithmetic-bus counter=transfer-bus counter?	08
07 GOTO (Wait)	06
08 Advance arithmetic-bus counter	09
09 GOTO	01

Table 2.5 Arithmetic-Bus Counter Control

Decision	No, next decision
01 Is instruction a floating-point fetch/store?	06
02 Is instruction a floating-point store?	06
03 Is forward/combine register a memory address?	10
04 Will memory bus accept operand?	04
05 Transmit operand to memory bus	06
06 Does store-check counter=arithmetic-bus counter?	08
07 GOTO	06
08 Advance store-check counter	09
09 GOTO	01
10 Store data in index memory	11
11 Is index store complete?	11
12 GOTO	08

Table 2.6 Store-Check Counter Control

For each process, a 2-bit ring counter indicates the level of the ILU instruction register containing the current instruction. The processes contain interlocks so that instruction execution produces the same result as that of a sequential machine.

Serial Arithmetic Unit

The serial arithmetic unit (SAU) processes data up to 8-bits wide. Although instructions may specify data fields of fewer than eight bits, the SAU operates on 8-bit bytes. Decimal numbers are assumed to be at least four bits long. Binary numbers are assumed to be eight bits long. If necessary, a shorter field is stored for the last result.

The symmetry of the arithmetic and logical instruction sets is reflected in the design of the SAU (Figure 2.8). Two accumulator registers supply the first operand, and two internal registers supply the second operand. The use of two registers for each operand allows data bytes to cross word boundaries. Selection of each operand byte from two operand registers is accomplished with a pair of 2-level switches. Each first-level switch selects a 16-bit field from its operand register pair; each second-level switch selects an operand byte from its 16-bit field. The eight unused bits of each 16-bit field are forwarded to the output switch where one set is used to reassemble the output field.

Instruction modifier bits control whether the true or complement form of each operand byte is delivered to the logic unit and adder.

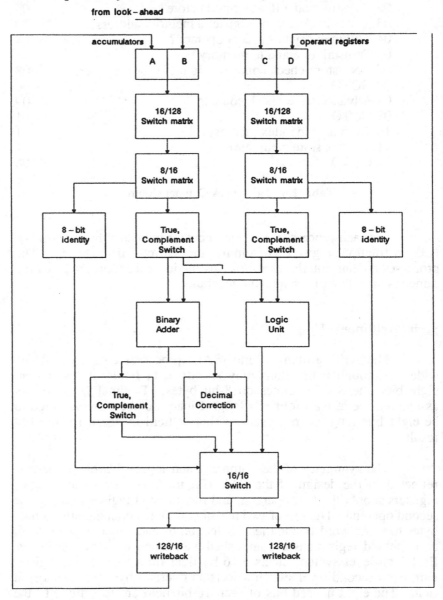

Figure 2.8 Serial Arithmetic Unit

The logic unit and adder operate in parallel. As specified by instruction modifier bits, the logic unit computes an arbitrary binary function of two variables. The adder produces an 8-bit binary sum of its two input operands. In binary mode, the sum may be complemented. Subtraction is performed using the appropriate combination of complement options for operands and result. In decimal mode, a correction must be applied to the binary sum produced by adding the internal codes of two decimal digits.

The internal codes of the decimal digits are:

Decimal Digit	Hex Code
0	60
1	62
2	64
3	66
4	68
5	6A
6	6C
7	6E
8	70
9	72

The representation of a decimal digit, n, is

$$R(n) = 96 + 2n,$$

and the binary sum of the representations of two decimal digits, n and m, is

$$R(n) + R(m) = 192 + 2(n + m) .$$

However, the representation of $n + m$ is

$$R(n + m) = 96 + 2(n + m) .$$

Thus, in decimal mode, two bit positions of the sum produced by the binary adder must be corrected.

The result byte is the output of either the logic unit or the binary adder. The binary adder output must be corrected in decimal mode, and optionally, may be complemented in binary mode. Depending on the instruction, the result byte will replace the input byte of either the first or second operand. The first stage of a 2-level switch reassembles the result byte and unused eight bits of the output operand into a 16-bit field. The second stage of the switch places the field into the appropriate output register.

Parallel Arithmetic Unit

The parallel arithmetic unit (PAU) processes floating-point data in single length or double length format. A carry-propagate adder (Figure 2.9) eliminates carry-ripple delay. Subtraction is performed by complementing the second operand. Normalization takes place in a shift unit capable of shifting four bits to the right or six bits to the left in one cycle.

Floating-point multiplication is performed in 3-bit subgroups, twelve bits at a time. Each 3-bit subgroup is decoded and generates a partial product. Except for the rightmost subgroup of the first group, the decoding requires only even multiples of the multiplier. As Figure 2.9 illustrates, no carries are present when the rightmost subgroup of the first group is decoded, allowing entry of the multiplicand when the multiplier is odd.

For example, subgroup k consists of bits $3k$-1, $3k$-2, and $3k$-3. Bit $3k$-3, if present, contributes a weight of -8 to subgroup k-1 (except for k=1, when the weight is +1 in subgroup 1). Bit $3k$-2 and bit $3k$-1 contribute weight 2 and 4 respectively. Bit $3k$, of subgroup k+1, contributes weight -8. For multiplier, M, possible partial products of subgroup k are: 2M, 4M, 6M, -2M, -4M, -6M, and 0.

Two carry-save adders combine the partial products of each group. The group sums are combined in subsequent carry-save adders while later groups are decoded and summed. The last iteration's partial product is forwarded to the carry-propagate adder to form the full product.

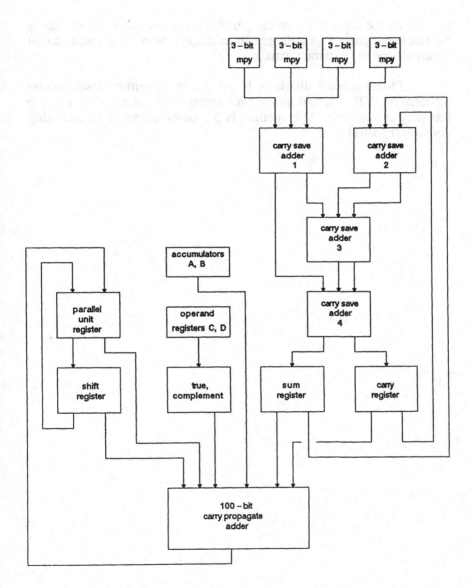

Figure 2.9 Parallel Arithmetic Unit

At the same time as the parallel arithmetic unit is calculating the fractional part of a floating-point multiply, the serial arithmetic unit is calculating the exponent part.

Floating-point divide is based on an algorithm described by Robertson [ROB58], and shifts over strings of ones or zeros up to 6 bits long at one time. This method is 3.5 times as fast as nonrestoring division [FRE61].

CHAPTER 3

THE CDC 6600

PERSPECTIVE

Although the present volume is exploring developments in computer architecture, the CDC 6600 is also noteworthy from several other points of view. Utilizing a novel approach to high density packaging and cooling, the system contained 400,000 silicon transistors. The result was a highly reliable system which became the standard of performance against which other scientific computers would be measured. As Thornton [THO70] points out, the CDC 6600 broke new ground in a number of areas by using:

1. Custom modules in place of building blocks;

2. Silicon transistors in place of germanium transistors;

3. Freon cooling in place of air cooling;

4. Multiple functional units;

5. Sixteen-fold interleaved memory units; and

6. Ten outboard I/O processors, each of which was a small, high speed computer specialized for data handling.

Items 1, 2, and 3 are technology-based and support, rather than extend, architectural decisions. Without these technological advances, it would not have been possible to implement the key architectural advances of the CDC 6600. The next sections examine these architectural developments individually.

ARCHITECTURE

The CDC 6600 is the first commercial computer system whose architecture addresses the difference in speed of the central processor, main memory, and input/output devices. The provision of multiple functional units allows processing to proceed somewhat independently of memory. Although the storage cycle time is greater than the central processor cycle time, the sixteen-way interleaved memory allows a sequence of consecutive operands to be fetched without encountering a delay. The peripheral processor units are small computer systems tasked with managing all aspects of an input/output request, leaving the central processor free for computational tasks (Figure 3.1).

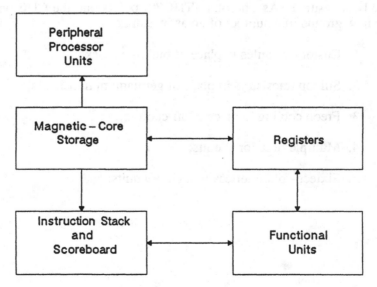

Figure 3.1 The CDC 6600

Registers

The CDC 6600 is a register-oriented machine. The central processor contains three sets of eight registers, specialized for addressing (A registers), for indexing (B registers), and for arithmetic/logical manipulation (X registers). The A and B registers, which deal with storage addresses, are 18 bits long. The X registers, which hold arithmetic operands, are 60 bits long.

Generally, floating-point data are loaded into the X registers, a sequence of arithmetic or logical operations is performed, and results are stored, thereby decoupling arithmetic processing from memory access time. This is especially important as the clock time of the CDC 6600 is 100 nanoseconds while the storage cycle time is 1 microsecond (1,000 nanoseconds). The B registers may be used for integer calculations, shift length control, and operations involving the exponent field of floating-point quantities (which combines aspects of integer calculations and shift control). The eight A registers are linked to their corresponding X registers. When an A register in the range A_1 through A_5 is modified, the corresponding X register is loaded with the contents of the memory location indicated by the A register. When A_6 or A_7 is modified, the contents of the corresponding X register are stored in the memory location indicated by the A register. A_0 and X_0 are not coupled, allowing their use for temporary values.

Instruction Format

The CDC 6600 is a three-address machine. The provision of register sets and three-address instructions was a major departure from the architecture of the highly successful IBM 7090, then in widespread use. In order to minimize the impact, on instruction size, of the need to specify both operand and result addresses, two instruction formats were created. In the short form instruction (15 bits), the operation code field is 6 bits; the result field and the two operand fields are each 3 bits long. Short form instructions specify registers both for their operands and their results. Long form instructions are 30 bits long. The second operand field is 18 bits long and is used to specify the storage address of an operand or to hold an 18-bit operand. Figure 3.2 illustrates the instruction formats.

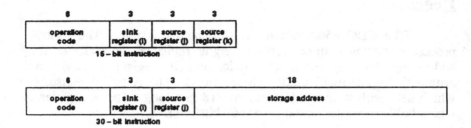

Figure 3.2 Instruction Formats

Multiple Functional Units

Labelled "functional parallelism" by Thornton [THO70], the provision of ten functional units permits a program to initiate a sequence of operations in consecutive cycles, without waiting for prior (independent) operations to complete. The ten functional units are: (a) boolean, (b) branch, (c) divide, (d) fixed add, (e) floating add, (f) increment (two units), (g) multiply (two units), and (h) shift.

Boolean Unit. The boolean unit produces a result in three cycles. It can perform three boolean functions of two operands: (a) and, (b) exclusive or, and (c) or. The identity function is implemented by transmitting the value of the second operand to a result register.

Each of these functions may be performed using either the true value of the second operand or the complemented value of the second operand.

Branch Unit. After a successful branch, the branch unit restores the status of the instruction stack. The instruction stack is an eight-word buffer which decouples the issuing of instructions from delays in accessing memory. This is especially important when a store instruction is contained in a small loop. The branch unit adjusts the instruction stack parameters so that, when execution resumes after a successful branch whose target address is within the instruction stack, the stack appears as if no branch had occurred.

Divide Unit. The divide unit is responsible for carrying out three operations: (a) floating divide, (b) rounded floating divide, and (c) population count (number of 1-bits in the operand).

The two floating-point divide operations each require 29 cycles; the population count requires 8cycles. The divide circuitry calculates the quotient 2 bits at a time by simultaneously subtracting the divisor, twice the divisor, and three times the divisor and then selecting the largest subtraction which does not change the sign. Calculation of the 48-bit quotient mantissa requires 24 cycles. Five cycles are used for calculation of the exponent.

The population count circuitry employs a 5-stage tree. The first stage computes the number of ones in each of seven 8-bit segments and one 4-bit segment. Stages two through five combine pairs of 4-bit sums into 5-, 6-, 7-, and, finally, 8-bit sums.

Fixed-Add Unit. The fixed-point add unit computes the one's complement sum or difference of two 60-bit operands. A carry-propagate adder minimizes total add time. The fixed-add unit also provides support to the branch unit by reporting on operand status: (a) equal zero, (b) less than zero, (c) greater than zero, (d) in range, (e) out of range, (f) definite, and (g) indefinite.

The latter four tests (range, definite) check the input bus for flags and are not computations based on arithmetic values.

Floating-Add Unit. The floating-add unit operates by determining the operand with the smaller exponent and then right shifting it by the difference of the exponents. This aligns the two operands' binary points. The shift network is simplified to exploit the fact that:

1. Only right shifts are performed.

2. Shifts of 64 or beyond (those requiring a 7-bit count field) yield zero for the shifted operand.

Addition of the aligned operands proceeds in a fashion similar to that of the fixed-point adder. After the addition, the sum is shifted so that it is normalized, and the exponent is adjusted by the shift count.

Increment Unit. There are two increment units which each handle three sets of instructions differing only in specification of the result register (A, B, or X register). Operations involving indexing, fixed-point calculations, and miscellaneous activities are directed to the B and X registers. Operations involving storage references are directed to the A registers. As described earlier, when an A register in the range A_1 through A_5 is altered, data from the storage location pointed to by the A register is transferred to the corresponding X register . When A_6 or A_7 is altered, a store operation transfers data from the corresponding X register to the storage location pointed to by the A register.

The various increment instructions are given below:

$A_j + K$ to A_k	30-bit instruction
$A_j + K$ to $?_i$	30-bit instruction
$B_j + K$ to $?_i$	30-bit instruction
$X_j + K$ to $?_i$	30-bit instruction
$X_j + B_k$ to $?_i$	15-bit instruction
$A_j + B_k$ to $?_i$	15-bit instruction
$A_j - B_k$ to $?_i$	15-bit instruction
$B_j + B_k$ to $?_i$	15-bit instruction
$B_j - B_k$ to $?_i$	15-bit instruction

Where ? is either an A, B, or X register.

The increment unit provides support to the branch unit for conditional jumps (comparable to the support provided by the fixed-add unit) in the following cases:

Go to $K + B_i$

Go to K when $B_i = B_j$

Go to K when $B_i = B_j$

Go to K when $B_i > B_j$

Go to K when $B_i < B_j$

The implementation of the increment unit is similar to that of the fixed-point adder. The sign is extended from the 18th bit when necessary.

Multiply Unit. The two (identical) multiply units can produce either a single or double precision product (in ten cycles or eleven cycles, respectively), or a rounded single precision product (in ten cycles). The advantages of three disparate techniques are obtained within a single multiply unit by:

1. Treating the 48-bit multiplier as two independent 24-bit multipliers and performing both 24-bit multiplications simultaneously;

2. Coding the multiplier bits two at a time and operating on them pairwise; and

3. Using a carry-save adder to compute the sum of each 24-bit multiply.

The 48-bit multiplier is split into two 24-bit multipliers. Each 24-bit multiplier is treated as a twelve digit base-4 number (e.g. twelve 2-bit quantities). Twelve partial products are formed by adding zero, one, two, or three times the multiplicand (depending on the multiplier's base-4 digit). The multiplicand is shifted two positions after each addition. Carries resulting from these additions are saved until the next addition cycle and combined at that time. Carries from the twelfth (final) addition iteration are handled when the two 24-bit multiplier products are combined. Thus, carry propagation is hidden at the cost of a small amount of extra logic. The result is a high speed multiplier with speed advantages outweighing the cost of additional circuitry.

Shift Unit.   The shift unit is used to perform several related instructions:

1. Set X_i to X_i shifted left/right by jk places.

2. Set X_i to X_k shifted left/right B_j places, where the direction is reversed when B_j is negative.

3. Set X_i to normalized (rounded) X_k and place into B_j the number of bits shifted.

4. Set X_i and B_j to the fraction and exponent parts of X_k (unpack).

5. Set X_i to the floating point number with exponent from B_j and fraction from X_k (pack).

6. Set X_i to $2^{(jk)}-1$ (create a mask of length jk bits, where jk represents a two-digit octal number).

The normalize instruction forms a count of the required left shift and places it into B_j and the control field of the shift register. Processing continues as in the shift left instruction. The normalize instruction requires four cycles. All other shift functions require three cycles.

Memory System

Interleaving.   There is a 10:1 mismatch between central memory speed (1,000 nanoseconds) and central processor speed (100 nanoseconds). Possible approaches to minimize delays due to this speed difference include:

1. Providing an intermediate memory between central memory and the central processor;

2. Minimizing storage references by architectural means (e.g. provide more register space); and

3. Increasing the storage bandwidth by transferring more data per unit time either by increasing the width of the data path or by allowing multiple overlapping data references (interleaving).

The IBM 7090 has only two registers, the accumulator and the multiplier/quotient, for holding intermediate values. In contrast, the CDC 6600 has a register-oriented instruction set and has a relatively large number (24) of registers. Other than load and store instructions, there are no arithmetic or logical instructions which deal with storage. All computations are performed upon quantities in the registers. Although large (multiple word) memory widths were considered as a means of increasing memory bandwidth, they were deemed incompatible with the requirement to access individual words of data in random order.

Memory interleaving provides increased bandwidth for randomly addressed operands and maximum bandwidth for sequences of consecutive operands. Furnishing the central processor with an instruction stack, which holds several instructions per word, sharply reduces the number of memory accesses necessary to supply the instruction stream. Further, the instruction stack acts as a buffer, allowing instructions to be fetched in advance of delays caused by address conflicts.

Magnetic Core Storage. The CDC 6600 memory uses *coincident current* magnetic core storage. The storage medium for each bit is a ferrite core, a toroid (doughnut shape) of compressed iron oxide. Data are stored by magnetizing the cores in either of two orientations to record a one or a zero. Ferrite exhibits a high coercivity, and the orientation of the magnetic state switches only when a sufficiently strong magnetic field is applied. Data are read by applying a magnetic field in the orientation used to record a zero, and then by detecting, or failing to detect, a magnetic state transition. A transition indicates that a one was stored, and that the core's orientation is switched (to that of zero). Lack of a transition indicates that a zero is already stored. Reading a core leaves it magnetized in the zero orientation. It must be rewritten to restore its initial state. A typical timing cycle for reading core memory is shown in Figure 3.3.

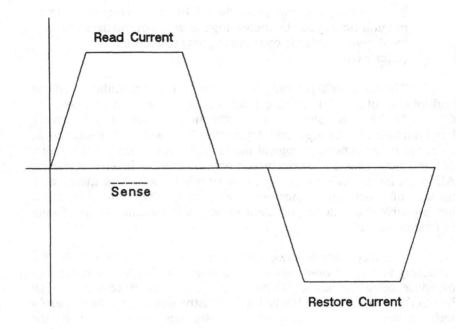

Figure 3.3 Core Memory Timing

Early magnetic core memories were limited by the need to have a separate wire for each core. The development of coincident-current core memory followed from the observation that magnetic state switching can be accomplished reliably when two half-level signals are present; yet, magnetic state switching will not occur when only one half-level signal is present. Taking advantage of this observation, a square array of n^2 cores can be addressed with only $2n$ drive lines (Figure 3.4), making the use of magnetic core practical. However, it imposes a time constraint. With only one drive line per word, switching time can be reduced by increasing drive current and the resulting magnetic field strength. This is not possible in coincident-current memories as the current in each drive-line must be less than that necessary to produce a transition. Reliability considerations further constrain circuit design to keep the current below this value. Thus, the magnetic field strength of a coincident-current memory has an upper bound of only twice that of the field strength necessary to cause a transition.

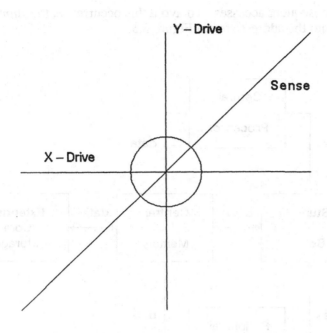

Figure 3.4 Magnetic Core Wiring

Organization. The CDC 6600's central memory is divided into 32 banks of 4,096 60-bit words. The total storage is 131,072 ($=2^{17}$) words and requires a 17-bit address field. The low order five bits select the bank, and the high order twelve bits select the word within a bank. Consecutive words of memory reside in different banks. Thus, up to 32 accesses (either load or store) may be made before the first bank is accessed again. The memory cycle time may be up to 32 times greater than the processor cycle time without reducing the data stream-rate.

Unlike a fully sequential memory, where each access (load or store) must wait until all prior requests are satisfied, an interleaved memory (one divided into separate banks, each operating independently) is capable of responding to multiple requests at once. Actual response times are a function of specific access patterns. A conflict (reference to a busy bank of memory), although less likely, will delay subsequent accesses. To avoid this occurrence, the *stunt box* is inserted into the address stream Figure 3.5.

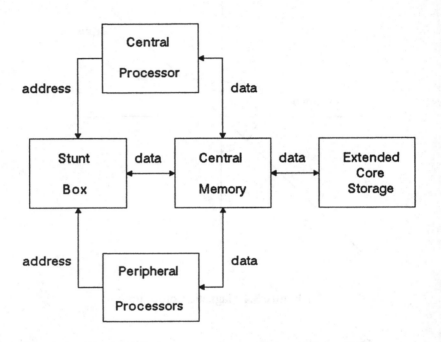

Figure 3.5 The Stunt Box

When a data address is presented, the stunt box checks to determine whether the appropriate memory bank is free. If so, the memory access is begun. If the bank is not free, the data address is recirculated within the stunt box. Up to three data addresses may be recirculated in the stunt box. This allows data to be accessed out of sequence, freeing the central processor from memory delays. In addition to the recirculating storage, the stunt box contains circuitry to prevent interchanging read and write accesses to the same location. For most data access patterns, the stunt box maximizes bandwidth between the central processor and storage.

Peripheral Processor Units

In early digital computer systems, the execution of I/O instructions was the responsibility of the central processor, which remained idle while data were transferred to, or from, a peripheral device. The development of I/O channels relieved the central processor of that task. Instead, the central processor created a list of I/O commands which was sent to the channel for execution. Although the central processor was free while data were transferred, it was still responsible for building the I/O command list and for controlling the peripheral equipment. If errors were detected during an I/O operation, the central processor attempted to recover any lost data.

The CDC 6600 is equipped with ten peripheral processor units (PPU) to carry out I/O and other external tasks. The central processor transmits an I/O request to a PPU and continues processing instructions. It is not involved with fulfilling the I/O request. The PPU interrupts the central processor at the conclusion of the I/O request.

The PPUs are small, high-speed processors, each with its own memory. The word size is twelve bits, and the memory contains 4,096 (2^{12}) words. Design of the PPUs took advantage of the 10:1 mismatch between memory cycle time and circuit speed. A hardware time-sharing mechanism, the *barrel*, permits sharing of logic, arithmetic, and control circuitry among the PPUs. The entire state of a PPU is described in 51 bits. The barrel holds the state of each PPU and provides each, in rotation, with its current state and a 100 nanosecond time slice. The PPUs appear to the central processor as ten separate processors, each with a 1,000 nanosecond cycle time.

INSTRUCTION PROCESSING

The instruction processing controls of the CDC 6600 are designed to maximize the rate at which instructions are executed. This approach depends on:

1. Multiple functional units which operate in parallel;

2. A sufficient number of processor registers to hold addresses and data so that the processor is decoupled from memory;

3. An *instruction stack* which serves to provide more rapid access to instructions; and

4. The *scoreboard*, a data traffic control, which manages the routing of data among the registers and functional units.

The Instruction Stack

The instruction stack, shown in Figure 3.6, consists of eight 60-bit registers which hold the instructions most recently executed. As instructions are fetched, they are sent to the stack's input register. Before the input is accepted, the contents of the stack are shifted to the next higher register position. The stack maintains a history of the most recently executed instructions.

A branch which transfers control back to an instruction in the stack, results in delivery of subsequent instructions from the stack. This results in several performance advantages:

1. There are no storage conflicts, as a storage cycle is not initiated.

2. Stack access time is shorter than storage access time.

3. The relative address (RA) and the central memory address need not be combined to yield an absolute memory location.

4. A central memory reference is omitted, reducing potential memory conflicts for data access.

The Scoreboard. The scoreboard is designed to allow each instruction to be issued as soon as possible. If a functional unit or result register is not available, then an instruction cannot be issued. Subsequent instructions may be issued provided that there are no result register or functional unit conflicts. As prior direct conflicts are resolved, the scoreboard allows issue of those instructions which were bypassed.

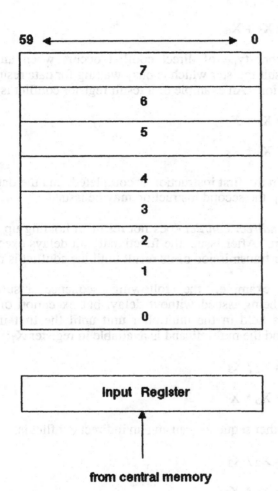

Figure 3.6 The Instruction Stack

Instruction Issue Conflicts. A *direct conflict* occurs when an instruction requires a functional unit which is busy due to a previously issued instruction. In the following example, both instructions use the add functional unit. The second instruction cannot be issued until the first instruction is completed, and the add unit is available:

$$X_1 = X_2 + X_3$$

$$X_4 = X_5 + X_6$$

Another type of direct conflict occurs when an instruction requires a result register which is busy waiting for data resulting from a prior instruction. An example of a result register conflict is:

$$X_1 = X_2 + X_3$$

$$X_1 = X_4 * X_5$$

When the first instruction is completed, and the data are stored in register X_1, the second instruction may be issued.

An *indirect conflict* does not result in holding up the issue of an instruction. After issue, the functional unit delays execution of the instruction or transmission of its result until the conflict is resolved.

For example, the following sequence results in both instructions being issued without delay, but execution of the second instruction is held in the multiplier unit until the first instruction is completed and the multiplicand is available in register X_1:

$$X_1 = X_2 / X_3$$

$$X_4 = X_5 * X_1$$

Another sequence causing an indirect conflict is:

$$X_1 = X_2 / X_3$$

$$X_4 = X_5 * X_1$$

$$X_5 = X_6 + X_7$$

In this case, the result of the third instruction must be held in the add function unit until the operand in register X_5 has been sent to the multiply function unit. By themselves, the second and third instructions would not result in a conflict. However, following the lengthy divide instruction, the result of the addition is ready to be stored into register X_5 before the multiply has begun. The indirect conflict on availability of register X_1 gives rise to a (store) conflict on register X_5. Register store conflicts are handled by holding the result in the functional unit until the conflict is resolved.

Register and Functional Unit Reservation and Release.
When an instruction is issued, the appropriate functional unit is marked busy, and the operand (input) and result (output) registers' designators are sent to the functional unit.

If an input register of one functional unit is reserved as the output register of another, then that functional unit's identifier is copied to the using functional unit. The current functional unit's identifier is placed with its output register, enabling subsequent copying as described in the prior sentence.

To begin an operation, both input operands must be flagged "ready". If an input operand register is marked to receive the result of a prior operation (including a read storage operation), the current operation must wait until the register is flagged "ready". This is accomplished one cycle after the prior operation concludes and stores its result. In the event that several functional units can complete simultaneously, a priority circuit is used to effect only one completion per cycle.

CHAPTER 4

THE IBM 360-91

PERSPECTIVE

The IBM 360 series of computers, introduced in 1964, is a family of systems covering a wide range of speed. From the perspective of a programmer, all models of the series share a common instruction set architecture and are compatible. The technology used to implement different models varies widely, as does the architectural approach. Low end, small machines have narrow data paths (8-bits wide), sequential functional units, and slow components. High end systems have 64-bit wide data paths, pipelined 64-bit wide functional units, and high speed logic. Additionally, the top of the line systems, the IBM 360-91 and 95 central processors employed a highly sophisticated look-ahead, pipeline/overlap system for improving performance in a manner transparent to the programmer. Many of the features of these systems, such as forwarding, combining, and the floating-point multiply strategy, were taken directly from the IBM Stretch.

The IBM 360/91 and 360/95

The IBM 360 series of computers, announced in 1964, represented a radical departure in product line. All models of computers within the IBM 360 family would be functionally compatible. That is, they would all have the same instruction set and, except for time dependencies, would be able to execute the same set of programs. Although the instruction set was the same for the entire family of computer systems, implementation differed from model to model. Lower models represented entry level systems for new users with small tasks. Mid-range models were aimed at providing the most cost-effective computing capability and were targeted at IBM's competition. Models at the high end of the family, the model 75, model 91, and model 95 were oriented to scientific and engineering use. Combining high speed and large memory, they offered users the possibility of addressing problems beyond the capabilities of other systems of the era. The model 91 and model 95 remained the highest speed computers marketed by IBM for over a decade.

The model 91 had a conventional core memory with a 750 nanosecond cycle time. The model 95 had a thin-film memory with a 120 nanosecond cycle time. We will refer only to the model 91 except where the difference is relevant. The model 91 attained its high speed through an approach emphasizing four areas:

1. Circuit technology utilized transistor switches which operated at speeds of less than 3 nanoseconds.

2. Packaging and cooling supported the requirements of high component density coupled with high power.

3. High speed algorithms were implemented for floating-point arithmetic.

4. Extensive concurrency hid delays caused by the disparity between the speeds of processor and storage.

ARCHITECTURE

The model 91 inherits its instruction set architecture from the IBM 360 family. The processor is register oriented, with most processing taking place on operands within registers. Storage is segmented into units of bytes (eight bit fields), half words (two bytes), full words (four bytes), and double words (eight bytes). Storage is addressed by byte, and each type of storage access must occur at an address which is a multiple of the basic data unit. That is, a double word must be located on a byte address which is a multiple of eight. A full word must be located at a byte address which is a multiple of four, and a half word must be located at a byte address which is a multiple of two.

Program Status Word

The program status word is eight bytes long and holds the dynamic state of the machine. It includes the: (a) instruction counter; (b) condition code; (c) program mask, which defines whether certain program interrupts will be recognized; (d) system mask, which defines which input/output interrupts will be recognized; (e) problem/supervisor state indicator, which controls the level of privilege granted to programs; (f) storage key, which must match the storage lock for a storage access to be completed; and (g) wait bit, which suspends instruction processing until an interrupt occurs.

Condition Code

Although part of the program status word, the condition code merits a separate description and discussion. Two bits long, the condition code is set after most instructions which perform arithmetic, logical, test, or input/output operations. It is not affected by data movement instructions such as load, store, or move character.

The 2-bit condition code indicates one of four states, with meanings specific to each instruction class. The branch instructions may specify any combination of the four possible states.

Registers

There are two sets of programmer-addressable registers: general purpose and floating point. The register sets are separate from one another. Operands are transferred between registers belonging to different register sets only by an indirect method which requires a store and a subsequent load.

General Purpose Registers. There are sixteen full-word (4 bytes) general-purpose registers. The general-purpose registers have four major uses.

First, they hold operands for, and results of, fixed-point and logical operations. Fixed-point operations may be full-word length, using the entire 4-byte register width, or they may be half-word length, using operands only two bytes wide. Results are always placed in registers in full-word format. The number system used for fixed-point arithmetic is two's complement. The ability to extend the sign bit of a two's complement number allows full-word arithmetic and half-word arithmetic to be intermixed.

Second, the general purpose registers serve as index registers. Instructions which permit indexing modify the storage address by adding the contents of the specified register to the storage address, yielding the effective address. If the index register field specified is zero, no indexing is performed. Register zero cannot participate in indexing operations.

General purpose registers are also used as base registers. The address space of the IBM 360 family is specified as 2^{24} bytes, or 16 megabytes. Although only the high-end models are offered with storage capacities exceeding a megabyte, compatibility requires the entire family of machines to provide for this large address space. The solution chosen by IBM is to provide a *base address* in a general purpose register, to be added to an offset field in each instruction. Although analogous to index registers, base registers typically remain static for long sequences of instructions.

The final major use of general-purpose registers is to hold the return address of subroutine linkage instructions. Using registers rather than core storage allows the creation of reentrant programs which can be interrupted and shared among several users. The registers are generally stored (by a single instruction) upon entry to a subroutine and restored at its conclusion.

Floating-Point Registers. There are four double-word (8-byte) floating-point registers numbered 0, 2, 4, and 6. They are only available to floating-point instructions. Data transfers between the floating-point registers and the general-purpose registers must use main memory as an intermediary. Single and double precision operations use the same registers. The low-order thirty-two bits do not participate in single precision operations and remain unchanged.

Instruction Format

The IBM 360 utilizes a two-address instruction. The first operand location (register or storage) is also the location of the operation result. There are four basic instruction types: register to register, register to storage, storage to storage, and storage-immediate. Instructions are two, four, or six bytes in length. Instruction length is determined by the operation code. In accord with the general storage alignment philosophy of the IBM 360, instructions may only begin at even numbered byte addresses.

Register to Register. The register to register instruction format is two bytes long (Figure 4.1). The first byte contains the eight bit operation code. The second byte holds two 4-bit fields: the first field designates the operand 1/result register; the second field designates the operand 2 register.

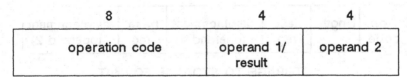

8	4	4
operation code	operand 1/ result	operand 2

REGISTER TO REGISTER FORMAT

Figure 4.1 Register to register instruction format

Register to Storage. The register to storage instruction format is 4 bytes long (Figure 4.2). As in the register to register format, the first byte contains the 8-bit operation code. The second byte holds two 4-bit fields: the first field designates the operand 1/result register; the second field designates the index register. The next two bytes hold the base/displacement fields. The first four bits specify the base register, and the remaining twelve bits specify a displacement. The effective storage address is obtained by adding the displacement (0-4095) to the contents of the specified base register (or zero if register zero is specified) and to the contents of the specified index register (or zero if register zero is specified). There is no functional difference between the base and the index register in this instruction.

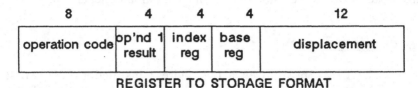

REGISTER TO STORAGE FORMAT

Figure 4.2 Register to storage instruction format

Storage to Storage. Storage to storage instructions are six bytes long (Figure 4.3). The first byte again contains the 8-bit operation code. The second byte indicates the operand length which may be 1-256 bytes. The next two bytes contain the operand 1/result storage address in base/displacement form. The last two bytes contain the operand 2 storage address in base/displacement form. Indexing is not available for this instruction type.

8	8	4	12	4	12
op code	length	base reg	displacement (operand 1)	base reg	displacement (operand 2)

STORAGE TO STORAGE FORMAT

Figure 4.3 Storage to storage instruction format

Storage-Immediate. The storage-immediate instructions are two bytes long (Figure 4.4). The first byte contains the eight bit operation code. The second byte holds the immediate data. These are the actual data, not a pointer to a register. Hence, the name used is *immediate*. The next two bytes specify a storage address in base/displacement form. Indexing is not available for storage-immediate instructions.

Storage-immediate instructions can perform either a test or a logical operation. If a test is specified, the immediate data are used as a "mask" to examine the byte at the effective storage address. The condition code indicates whether none, some, or all of the bits specified by the mask were 1-bits. If a logical operation is specified, the immediate data are used as operand 2, and the byte at the effective address is used as the operand 1/result. The condition code indicates whether the result of the logical operation is zero or non-zero.

8	8	4	12
op code	Immediate data	base reg	displacement

STORAGE – IMMEDIATE FORMAT

Figure 4.4 Storage-immediate instruction format

Instructions

The IBM 360 and its descendants, the IBM 370 and IBM 30xx series, are ubiquitous. Their rich instruction set does not need detailed explanation in this volume. Instead, the following paragraphs briefly summarize the fixed-point and floating-point operations upon which the hardware of the 360/91 is focused.

Floating-point arithmetic. The floating-point instructions operate on 32-bit (single-precision) or 64-bit (double-precision) quantities. Separate instructions are provided for combinations of options. Up to eight variations are possible for some of the floating-point instructions.

In the list which follows, the instruction modifiers are as given below:

R/X: Specifies the location of the second operand (R=register, S=storage).

S/D: Specifies whether the operation is carried out in single precision or double precision, (S=single, D=double).

N/U: Specifies normalized or unnormalized arithmetic, (N=normalized, U=unnormalized).

(C/I/N/P) Specifies the format of the operand to be transmitted, (C=complemented, I=identity, N=negative, P=positive).

The following floating-point arithmetic operations are available:

Add/Subtract (R/X, S/D, N/U): Set the first operand register to the sum/difference of the first operand and second operand values. Set the condition code.

Multiply (R/X, S/D): Set the first operand register to the product of the first and second operand values.

Divide (R/X, S/D): Set the first operand register to the quotient of the first and second operand values.

The following floating-point instructions transmit a value and/or set the condition code:

Load (R/X, S/D): Transmit the value of the second operand to the first operand register.

Store (S/D): Transmit the value in the first operand register to the second operand storage location.

Compare (R/X, S/D): Set the condition code to reflect the comparison of the first and second operand values.

Load and Test (C/I/N/P): Transmit the value of the second operand register to the first operand register. Set the condition code to reflect the result value.

Fixed-point and logical operations. Separate fixed-point instructions are used when an operation can be used with either 32-bit (full-word) or 16-bit (half-word) quantities. When there is a choice of full-word, half-word, or logical (unsigned) arithmetic, the modifiers F, H, and L are used. The modifier, M, is used when a sequence of values may be transmitted.

The following fixed-point and logical operations are available:

Add/Subtract (R/X, F/H/L): Set the first operand register to the sum/difference of the first operand and second operand values. Set the condition code.

Multiply (R/X, F/H): Set the first operand register to the product of the first and second operand values.

Divide (R/X): Set the first operand register to the quotient of the first and second operand values.

Boolean (R/X): Set the first operand register to the result of the specified boolean operation on the first and second operand values. The boolean operations are: (a) and, (b) or, and (c) exclusive or.

The following fixed-point instructions transmit a value, or set the condition code:

Load (R/X, F/H/M): Transmit the value of the second operand to the first operand register.

Store (F/H/M): Transmit the value in the first operand register to the second operand storage location.

Compare (R/X, F/H/L): Set the condition code to reflect the comparison of the first and second operand values.

Load and Test (C/I/N/P): Transmit the value of the second operand register to the first operand register. Set the condition code to reflect the result value.

IMPLEMENTATION PHILOSOPHY

The performance goal for the IBM 360 Model 91 was to attain a speed approaching 100 times that of the IBM 7090. Technology could only provide a factor of approximately four (from 20 nanoseconds to approximately 5 nanoseconds). The remaining factor of twenty would have to be attained through machine organization. Improved floating-point algorithms would provide some of the speed increase. The remainder of the increase would have to be achieved through increased concurrency. In order to simplify the design problem, the machine was organized as a set of loosely coupled, autonomous units: (a) instruction unit, (b) fixed-point unit, (c) floating-point unit, (d) main storage control element, and (e) peripheral storage control element. Within each unit, pipelining is used to allow the maximum hiding of latency and delay.

The requirement to be a compatible member of the IBM 360 family was a significant complication. Strict compatibility was not achieved. In three circumstances, the model 91 produces different results than other IBM 360 models.

1. The quotient of a floating-point division may differ by one bit in the least significant digit. The result on the model 91 is slightly more accurate than the result produced on the rest of the IBM 360 models. The model 91 division algorithm yields a remainder with magnitude less than half the divisor. The division performed on a standard IBM 360 yields a remainder between zero and the divisor.

2. Decimal instructions are not implemented. A *program interrupt* is generated if a decimal instruction is attempted. An interrupt servicing routine simulates the decimal instruction and returns to the user program. This approach is transparent to the user.

3. Input/output instructions may return a condition code value not possible on other models. The model 91 is sufficiently fast, permitting an I/O instruction in an interrupt handler to find different conditions than those seen by other processors.

The major-cycle time was determined by considering the tradeoff between attaining increased concurrency via more stages, and incurring increased cost and complexity with the additional levels of control circuitry required to manage a longer pipeline. Additionally, each level of pipeline requires a buffer latch which introduces a small additional delay. The delay imposed by this latch results in a maximum pipeline length which, if exceeded, would cause the machine to be slowed down.

Extensive buffering is provided within the functional units so that delays between the units cause minimal disruption in processing flow. Thus, storage access time, branch instructions, condition code testing, and lengthy floating-point instructions are overlapped with other functions.

INSTRUCTION UNIT

The instruction unit performs the initial processing for every instruction, forwarding fixed-point and floating-point instructions to the appropriate functional unit for execution. The instruction unit is responsible for executing a large assortment of miscellaneous instructions including branch, storage to storage, immediate, status switching, and input/output instructions.

Typical program sequences require a branch every few instructions [KNU70]. This has the effect of introducing a discontinuity and delay into the instruction stream. At the same time, floating-point instructions, particularly multiply and divide, are lengthy. The variability of these two processes suggests that the instruction unit, which supplies instructions to the floating-point unit, on average must be capable of providing instructions to the floating-point unit at a high rate. This results in a backlog of instructions available to the floating-point unit, so that when a delay (e.g. a branch) arises, the floating-point unit continues processing until the instruction unit recovers.

Instruction Fetch

The goal of the instruction fetch mechanism is to assure that future instructions are available for processing as required. An instruction buffer is provided for holding instructions fetched in advance of need. This eight double-word buffer, the instruction stack, is also used to smooth out disturbances caused by branch instructions and to minimize instruction fetches for loops.

The same memory access mechanism is used for instruction fetch as for operands. The use of a single path allows sharing of control hardware and permits storage access conflicts to be resolved simply. When the number of instructions in the instruction buffer is below the current threshhold, memory access conflicts are resolved in favor of instruction fetch. Otherwise, they are resolved in favor of operand fetch. Table 4.1 describes the instruction fetch algorithm.

Decision	No, next decision
01: Sequential ins'n fetch allowed?	Wait
02: Is this initial start?	06
03: First two double words fetched?	05
04: GOTO	06
05: Fetch first two double words.	06
06: Next ins'n buffer slot available?	Wait
07: Prior fetch request accepted?	Wait
08: Is loop mode set?	11
09: Is instruction buffer full?	16
10: GOTO	09
11: Fetched 3 double words in advance?	16
12: Storage busy with operand fetch?	14
13: GOTO	12
14: Fetched 4 double words in advance?	16
15: GOTO	14
16: Fetch next double word	01
17: GOTO	01

Table 4.1 Instruction fetch control

Instruction Buffer Array

The instruction buffer array and instruction fetch mechanism decouple instruction supply from instruction processing. When the instruction stream is sequential, the instruction fetch mechanism operates as described above. The instruction fetch mechanism attempts to maintain a supply of instructions in the instruction buffer in advance of need. Figure 4.5 depicts the instruction buffer array and related data paths.

Branch Instructions. The appearance of a branch instruction signals a point in the instruction stream where sequential flow may be altered. A successful branch causes the startup of a new instruction stream sequence. If the target address of the branch is not already contained in the instruction buffer, then the processing of the new stream of instructions will be repeatedly delayed by storage access cycles until the instruction buffer is replenished. Branch instructions occur so frequently that it was deemed necessary to minimize the disruption they cause.

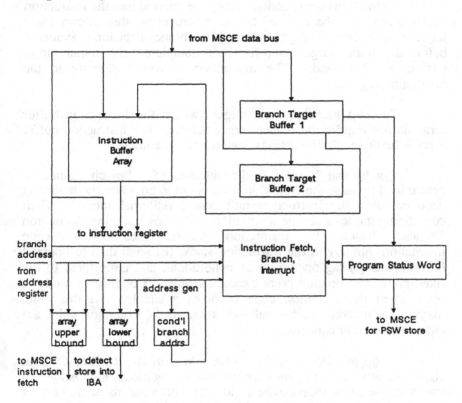

Figure 4.5 Instruction buffer array

If the condition code is not valid when a branch instruction is encountered, the instruction unit sets *conditional mode* and continues decoding instructions and issuing them to the fixed-point and floating-point execution units.

Branch Target Processing.   Two additional double words, branch target buffer 1 and branch target buffer 2, shown in Figure 4.5, contain the beginning of a branch's target instruction stream. This allows instruction processing to proceed while the instruction buffer array is replenished. Although this approach adds some overhead to branches which fail, it markedly reduces delay for branches which succeed.

Instructions are decoded as they are entered into the instruction buffer array. In the case of branch instructions, this allows early fetching to the branch target buffers. If the branch decision is available before the branch target fetch has been completed, the branch target buffers are bypassed. The instruction is routed directly to the instruction register.

Forward branches with targets within the instruction buffer array do not require the branch target buffers. The instruction buffer array is loaded with instructions from the target address.

Conditional Mode. If the outcome of a branch cannot be determined because the condition code is not valid when the branch is decoded, then the instruction unit sets conditional mode. When conditional mode is set the instruction unit stops initiating instruction fetches. Instead, the instruction unit continues to (a) decode instructions already in the instruction stack; (b) fetch data to operand buffers; and (c) tag operations as conditional, and issue them to the fixed-point and floating-point execution units. Conditional mode is reset when the condition code becomes available. At this time, instructions marked conditional and issued to the execution units, are either executed or cancelled.

Loop Mode. A *backward branch*, with target address within eight double words, triggers a special processing mode, *loop mode*. In this case, the entire loop can be contained within the instruction buffer array. Based on the reasonable hypothesis that such loops are traversed more than one time, it is possible to attain several performance improvements. When loop mode is set, the instruction buffer array is filled, and instruction fetching is halted as long as loop mode remains set. The branch's target instruction is placed in the first double word, leaving the remaining space for those instructions immediately following the loop. The full storage bandwidth is available for operand fetching and storing, allowing a one instruction per cycle issue rate. Additionally, the backward branch, which set loop mode, is expected to succeed. (Normally branches are expected to fail.) This results in a large decrease in branch instruction time.

For example, most Fortran compiler-generated DO loops end with an instruction to increment and test the induction variable and to branch when the induction variable is at or below the final value, the BXLE instruction. Three cycles are necessary for a successful BXLE instruction in loop mode. When not in loop mode, eight cycles are required for a BXLE instruction.

Loops which end with data dependent conditional branches (not those from the index register family) also benefit from treatment of the branch as expected to succeed. In this case, subsequent instructions are issued conditionally. This means that operand fetches will occur, but functional unit execution will not occur until the branch is resolved. While the loop is active, this results in overlapping operand fetch with branch resolution. Only when the branch fails (on the last traversal of the loop) have extra operand fetches been performed.

The model 91 console has a loop mode indicator. Instrumentation reveals that loop mode is set for 25 to 40 per cent of the time. A major programming activity is rewriting loops to fit into the instruction buffer array. A loop's running time may decrease more than 30 per cent if it fits into the instruction buffer array.

Interrupt Handling. Interrupts are similar to branch instructions in their effect upon instruction stream processing. Unlike branches, they are generally asynchronous with respect to the instruction sequence, except for the *supervisor call* which is an instruction defined by the architecture to behave as an interrupt. Because the pipeline ordinarily will contain several instructions at various stages of execution, it is not possible to associate an interrupt with a particular instruction. This causes no difficulty for external events. However, interrupts caused by instruction execution must be flagged as *imprecise*. The pipeline is drained (emptied while further instruction processing is inhibited), and the interrupt is signaled as associated with the last instruction in the pipeline.

Imprecise interrupts are an addition to the IBM 360 architectural specification. These interrupts indicate that the event which caused the interrupt occurred within the last several instructions executed before the interrupted instruction. Because a branch instruction might have been executed, it is generally not possible to know with certainty the identity of the instruction causing the imprecise interrupt. The following conditions cause imprecise interrupts: (a) out of bounds addresses; (b) data misalignment; (c) storage access violations; and (d) arithmetic exceptions, such as overflow and divide by zero. In these cases, the program is generally terminated.

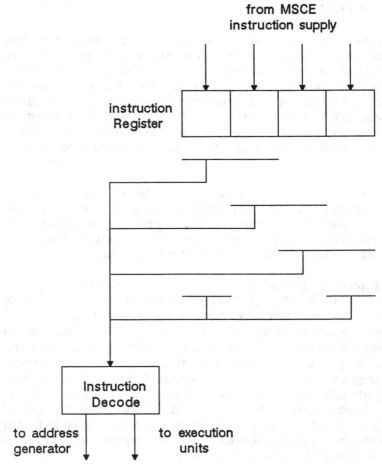

Figure 4.6 Instruction issue register

In order to minimize the interrupt time (which is unavoidably lengthy because of the requirement to drain the pipeline), the target of the post-interrupt instruction stream is loaded into the branch target buffers, and the interrupt is treated as a successful branch.

Instruction Issue

The instruction issue mechanism is designed to test each instruction for interlock conditions, to clear any interlocks, and to issue the instruction. To accommodate the variable length instruction format, the decode circuitry fetches half-word parcels from the instruction buffer array. The instruction issue register, shown in Figure 4.6, holds one double word and is used as an assembly register so that the operation code field will be consistently placed.

After a partial decode, instructions are checked for interlocks which must be cleared before they are issued. Asynchronous interlocks are set by: (a) the operator console (e.g. the stop button, the single instruction execute switch); (b) by interrupts (e.g. external, machine check, input/output); (c) the interval timer (during an update cycle); and (d) entering wait state. Further, instruction-dependent items are checked: (a) invalid operation code, (b) invalid instruction address (odd byte address), (c) address generation required (together with availability of the address adder), and (d) availability of fixed-point or floating-point execution unit resources. If errors are found, the appropriate interrupt sequence is begun. At this time, data dependent actions are also checked. If a branch was incorrectly predicted, a *fix up* must be performed. If a store to the instruction stream is found, the following instruction must not be processed until after the store has occurred.

Checking for a store into the instruction stream is one of the most complex tasks in the instruction issue process. (After the CDC 6600 was first installed, it's documentation had to be changed to describe the specific conditions when a store into the instruction stream would affect processing.) A full-width comparison of the store address with the boundaries of the instruction buffer array caused an unacceptable delay for each store instruction. To avoid this delay, only the low-order bits of the store address are checked. A test was sought which would be fast and would minimize the instances causing unnecessary delay. The chosen test ignores the low-order three bits (addressing bytes within a double word) and compares the next three bits (mod 8 address) with the corresponding bits of the current instruction address. A delay is signaled if any of the following conditions are met:

1. The store address matches the current instruction address. The probability is 1/8.

2. The current instruction continues into the next double word, and that address matches the store address. The probability is 1/16.

3. Address arithmetic causes a carry into the mod 8 address. This has a probability of 1/4 when full-word (4-byte) addressing is in use, and has a probability near zero when double-word (8-byte) addressing is in use. In double-word addressing mode, the base, displacement, and index values are generally multiples of eight. Consequently address-arithmetic carries will rarely occur in the low-order three bits.

FIXED-POINT EXECUTION UNIT

The fixed-point execution unit executes all fixed-point, logical, and variable field length operations (Figure 4.7). The major elements of the fixed-point execution unit are:

1. Sixteen general-purpose registers hold temporary values of logical and arithmetic operations.

2. Six fixed-point (single word) operand buffers receive data from storage and hold them until needed.

3. An operation stack buffers and holds up to six fixed-point instructions from the instruction unit.

4. The fixed-point functional unit and logical functional unit perform arithmetic and boolean operations.

5. The variable field length execution unit performs operations on variable field length data.

Fixed-Point and Logical Operations

The instruction unit initiates storage fetch requests for operands of fixed-point and logical operations. The operand buffers hold these data when they are received from storage. The instruction unit forwards fixed-point and logical instructions in register-to-register format. An operand buffer designator is used in place of the address designator of instructions which were originally in register-to-storage format.

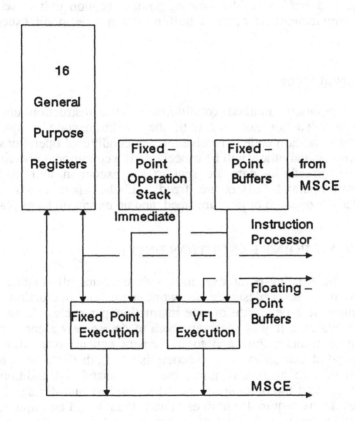

Figure 4.7 Fixed-point execution unit

Within the fixed-point execution unit, instruction processing proceeds serially through the operation stack. After decoding, an instruction can be executed if the required data and execution unit are available.   Decoding of the next instruction is overlapped with execution of the current instruction. In the case of multiple-operation instructions, decoding is delayed until the last operation has begun.

Variable Field Length Operations

Variable field length operations require many storage accesses. The operand buffers of the floating-point execution unit (discussed below) supplement the operand buffers of the fixed-point execution unit.

Conditional Mode

Operations marked conditional by the instruction unit are neither decoded nor executed until the condition code is resolved. When the condition code is resolved, some conditional operations will be performed and others will be cancelled. If a conditional operation is to be performed, its data are sent to the execution unit, and the associated operand buffers are freed.   If the operation is to be cancelled, its operand buffers are freed, and no execution takes place.

FLOATING-POINT EXECUTION UNIT

The floating-point execution unit executes all floating-point instructions.   It is designed to work with the instruction issue mechanism at a peak rate of one instruction per cycle. In order to achieve this rate, it was necessary both to devise new algorithms for floating-point operations and to implement concurrency within the floating-point execution unit. Accomplishing both these aims led to creation of two arithmetic units, one specialized for addition and subtraction, and the other specialized for multiply and divide. Fewer logic levels are required within each unit than would be required in a combination unit, and thus, each can be faster.   A floating-point instruction unit (FLIU) assigns each operation to the appropriate arithmetic unit.   The major elements of the floating-point execution unit (Figure 4.8) are:

1. Four floating-point (double-word) registers;

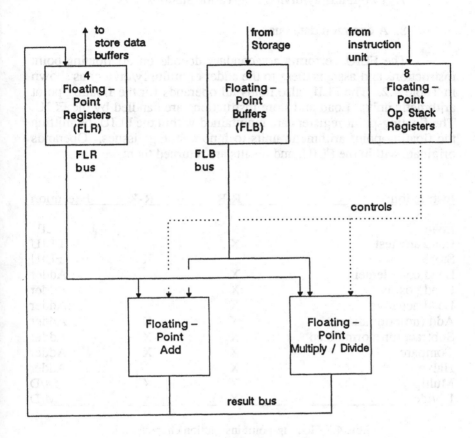

Figure 4.8 Floating-point execution unit

2. Six floating-point operand buffers;

3. Eight position (14 bits: operation code and register fields) operation stack;

4. A floating-point add unit;

5. Three adder reservation stations;

6. A multiply/divide unit;

7. Two multiply/divide reservation stations; and

8. A common data bus.

The FLIU performs a secondary decode on all floating-point instructions and assigns them to the adder or multiply/divider as shown in Table 4.2. The FLIU also holds all operands for the floating-point arithmetic units. Load and store instructions are handled by the FLIU. The floating-point registers are maintained within the FLIU, permitting the floating-point arithmetic units to ignore storage issues. Operands originate within the FLIU, and results are returned there.

Instruction	R-R	R-X	Execution
Load		X	FLIU
Load and test	X		FLIU
Store		X	FLIU
Load complement	X		Adder
Load positive	X		Adder
Load negative	X		Adder
Add (un)normalized	X	X	Adder
Subtract (un)normalized	X	X	Adder
Compare	X	X	Adder
Halve	X		Adder
Multiply	X	X	M/D
Divide	X	X	M/D

Table 4.2 Floating-point instruction characteristics

The FLIU processes a register-to-storage (RX) fetch instruction in three stages. First, it finds an available floating-point buffer. Then, it initiates a storage access to obtain the data. Finally, it substitutes the floating-point buffer number in the operand field of the instruction before sending it to the floating-point operation stack. Instructions are not delayed awaiting completion of the storage fetch cycle. The floating-point buffers indicate whether or not they have been loaded with requested data from storage. Store instructions are handled in a similar manner, using store data buffers to hold data until the data can be sent to storage. The outcome of these substitutions is that storage requests are handled as are any other requests made to functional units within the floating-point unit. All instructions are placed on the floating-point operation stack in a register-to-register (RR) format. The result register field indicates the (programmer specified) floating-point register containing the first operand. The source register field indicates a floating-point register or floating-point buffer containing the second operand. In the case of store instructions, the source register field indicates the store data buffer which holds the target storage address and which will hold the data to be stored.

The functional units operate in the mode of a dataflow processor. They begin an arithmetic operation when their controls indicate that required operands are present. The floating-point buffers forward data to the appropriate functional unit when they become full (i.e. when data arrive from storage). The store data buffer initiates a storage cycle when it receives data.

Conditional Mode

Operations marked conditional by the instruction unit are neither decoded nor executed until the condition code is resolved. If the operation is to be performed, data are sent to the execution unit, and associated operand buffers are freed. If the operation is cancelled, the operation buffers are freed, but no execution takes place.

Execution Unit Concurrency

The instruction fetch mechanism and the provision of separate floating-point and fixed-point execution units, each with its own register set, allows the concurrent execution of fixed and floating-point instructions. Dependencies between fixed-point and floating-point instructions do not occur except through storage accesses.

Dependencies among a sequence of floating-point operations are the norm. As the execution of floating-point instructions is quite lengthy, concurrency among them yields a significant performance advantage. Individual functional units are provided and optimized for each operation. Nonetheless, two cycles are required for addition; three cycles are required for multiply; and twelve cycles are required for division. The availability of separate functional units enables concurrent execution of floating-point operations. However, determining possible concurrency within the floating-point execution unit is complicated by the use of a single register set. It is necessary to take into account each instruction's reliance upon data from prior instructions. The common data bus (CDB) is a mechanism which unifies data transfers among the floating-point functional units and, through register and data tagging, allows a high degree of concurrency. The common data bus permits out-of-order instruction execution while preserving data dependencies.

Busy-bit Tagging. Prior to the development of the common data bus, a proposal was considered to tag the floating-point registers as busy to prevent their use in dependent instructions. This *busy bit* proposal has advantages of simplicity and minimal circuitry requirements, but does not provide the high levels of concurrency desired. It is described here to illustrate the considerations which led to the development of the full common data bus.

In the program fragment:

> LD 2,FLB3   Load floating register 2 from floating-point buffer 3 (which holds the storage data from an RX fetch instruction)
>
> AD 2,FLB1   Add FLB 1 to floating register 2

the addition cannot begin until the load is completed, and the data are available. Further, an operation cannot begin until its source register is no longer awaiting data from a prior operation. In contrast, in the program fragment:

> LD 2,FLB3   Load floating register 2 from FLB3 (from storage)
>
> AD 4,FLB5   Add FLB 5 into floating register 4

the addition is independent of floating register 2, and can begin whenever FLB 5 is available, even if that occurs before the load instruction is completed.

This illustrates the reliance on the programmer to choose instruction sequences which avoid dependencies. The program fragment below exhibits the effect of using a single register in a string of computations, causing each instruction to be dependent upon its immediate predecessor:

LD 0,E	Fetch E to floating register 0
AD 0,D	Fetch D, add to reg 0; (D + E)
MD 0,C	Fetch C, mpy reg 0; C * (D + E)
MD 0,B	Fetch B, mpy reg 0;
	B * C * (D + E)
MD 0,A	Fetch A, mpy reg 0;
	A * B * C * (D + E)

Restructuring such a maximum-height-tree into another form will yield opportunities for concurrent execution. A mechanism must be included to permit concurrency and, at the same time, to guard against execution sequences which would violate instruction precedence relationships of the sequential code.

A 1-bit field, the *busy bit*, is concatenated to each of the floating-point registers. Whenever the floating-point execution unit issues an operation (this is not the instruction issue which occurs at the instruction buffer array of the instruction unit), the busy-bit field of the result register is set. The busy bit is reset when the register receives the result. Instruction issuing stops upon reaching an instruction whose source register is tagged as busy or when the required functional unit is busy. This results in a limitation demonstrated by the program fragment which computes the expression A * B * C * (D + E):

1	LD 0,D	Fetch D to floating register 0
2	LD 2,C	Fetch C to floating register 2
3	LD 4,B	Fetch B to floating register 4
4	AD 0,E	Fetch E, add to reg 0; (D + E)
5	MD 2,0	C * (D + E)

6 MD 4,A   Fetch A, mpy register 4; (A * B)

7 MD 2,4   A * B * C * (D + E)

All seven instructions above are decoded and issued to the floating-point execution unit without delay by the instruction unit. Instructions one through three are independent and begin immediately. Although instruction four is dispatched for execution, its addition can not begin until both operands have arrived from storage. Register 0 is specified as a sink register; its busy-bit will be set. Instruction five specifies register 0 (now marked busy) as the source. It is dispatched, but can not proceed until instruction four completes and sends its result to register 0. Although instruction six is independent of both instructions four and five, it can not execute until the multiplier becomes available. Further, the idle multiplier unit is marked busy as it waits for register 0 (which will receive the result of instruction 4). When register 0 is available, the multiplier will execute and will become available. Instruction seven, also using the multiplier, must wait for the execution of instruction 6 to conclude.

Reservation Stations. The inclusion of additional arithmetic resources improves the situation, but not as much as at first expected. Each time execution is delayed due to register-busy status or arithmetic-unit-busy status, an additional delay (signalling the start of the operation) is incurred when the busy status is removed. Time is lost transmitting control status from functional unit to sink register, and then to waiting functional unit.

Providing multiple sets of buffers, termed "reservation stations," to hold control information and the source register and sink register fields, yields most of the advantages of additional functional units as well as reduces delays associated with transmission of control status. Reservation stations require significantly less hardware than functional units. There are three reservation stations for the add functional unit and two reservation stations for the multiply/divide functional unit. They allow decoding to continue when a reservation station is available, even though the functional unit may be busy or waiting.

An important limitation of the busy-bit/reservation station approach becomes apparent in the treatment of instructions within a loop. Within a loop, modifications to registers occurring at the end of one iteration will cause delays in accessing those registers in the next iteration. If a loop begins with load instructions, causing register usage between iterations to be independent, then it should be possible to proceed without delay. However, in the example below, the load instruction at the beginning of each iteration (and the following instructions) will be delayed until the prior iteration is completed. (Here and in the following example, the general format of IBM 360 assembly language will be followed. Technical details, such as byte alignment, which would obscure the purpose of the examples are omitted).

	L I,=1	Set I=1 to begin loop X
X	LD 0,E(I)	Fetch E_i to floating register 0
	AD 0,D(I)	Fetch D_i, add to reg 0; $(D_i + E_i)$
	MD 0,C(I)	Fetch C_i, mpy reg 0; $C_i * (D_i + E_i)$
	MD 0,B(I)	Fetch B_i, mpy reg 0; $B_i * C_i * (D_i + E_i)$
	MD 0,A(I)	Fetch A_i, mpy reg 0; $A_i * B_i * C_i * (D_i + E_i)$
	STD 0,F(I)	Store reg 0 in F_i
	BXLE I,30,1,X	DO I = 1,30,1 (back to X)

The compiler technique of loop unrolling can be used to decrease the delay by averaging it over several iterations. Unrolled, the loop becomes:

	L I,=1	Set I=1 to begin loop X
Y	LD 0,E(I)	Fetch E_i to floating register 0
	LD 2,E+1(I)	Fetch E_{i+1} to floating register 2
	AD 0,D(I)	Fetch D_i, add to reg 0; $(D_i + E_i)$
	AD 2,D+1(I)	Fetch D_{i+1}, add to reg 2; $(D_{i+1} + E_{i+1})$
	MD 0,C(I)	Fetch C_i, mpy reg 0; $C_i * (D_i + E_i)$

MD 2,C+1(I) Fetch C_{i+1}, mpy reg 2; $C_{i+1} * (D_{i+1} + E_{i+1})$

MD 0,B(I)   Fetch B_i, mpy reg 0; $B_i * C_i * (D_i + E_i)$

MD 2,B+1(I) Fetch B_{i+1}, mpy reg 2
$B_{i+1} * C_{i+1} * (D_{i+1} + E_{i+1})$

MD 0,A(I)   Fetch A_i, mpy reg 0;
$A_i * B_i * C_i * (D_i + E_i)$

MD 2,A+1(I) Fetch A_{i+1}, mpy reg 2
$A_{i+1} * B_{i+1} * C_{i+1} * (D_{i+1} + E_{i+1})$

STD 0,F(I)   Store reg 0 in F_i

STD 2,F+1(I) Store reg 2 in F_{i+1}

BXLE I,30,2,X   DO I = 1,30,2   (back to Y)

Thus, the loop has been unrolled into two copies per iteration. Now, computations may be performed concurrently for two values of the loop index, i and $i+1$. A delay remains at the beginning of each loop iteration, due to calculations of the previous iteration which have not yet completed . Performance of the unrolled loop is improved because the effective delay at the start of the loop (the delay divided by the number of index values computed per loop execution) is decreased, and the concurrency is increased by the pattern of alternating register usage. Further unrolling will decrease the effective delay at the start of the loop, but will cause the code to be too long to fit into the instruction buffer array and achieve loop mode. The resulting increase in branch overhead and instruction fetching interference will decrease performance.

The Common Data Bus

The common data bus (Figure 4.9) is a set of controls as well as a data path which connects to all elements which can send data to, or receive data from, the floating-point registers. In addition to its advantages in attaining floating-point instruction execution concurrency, the CDB provides a direct path to the registers from storage (e.g. for a load instruction). The prior design (Figure 4.8) required data to pass through a floating-point functional unit.

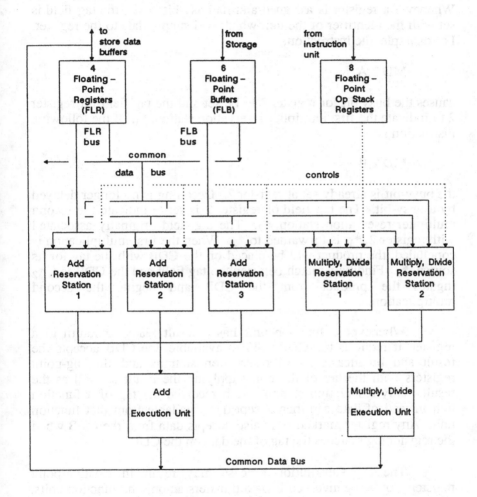

Figure 4.9 The common data bus

The CDB controls functional unit activity through *tags* which identify the source of data on the bus. Each data source is assigned a tag number. The data sources are the floating-point buffers (FLB$_i$), the adder reservation stations (*$_1$, *$_2$, and *$_3$), and the multiply/divide reservation stations ($*_1$, and $*_2$). To accommodate these 11 identifiers, the tag field must be 4 bits wide. A tag field is maintained with each element which can receive data from, or send data to, the CDB. Whenever a register is assigned and its busy-bit is set, the tag field is set with the identifier of the unit which will supply data to the register. For example, the instruction,

MD 2,A

causes the busy bit for register 2 to be set and the tag field for register 2 to indicate the first multiplier reservation station, $*_1$. If the following instruction is:

MD 2,B

the busy-bit is already set at register 2. Decoding is no longer delayed by a busy-bit. The tag field of register 2 is set to indicate the second multiplier reservation station, $*_2$. The tag field originally associated with register 2, $*_1$, is forwarded to $*_2$. When the first multiplication is concluded, the product will be placed on the CDB with the tag for its source, $*_1$. Finding a match between the tag field and the CDB tag, $*_2$ ingates the product from the CDB and begins the second multiplication.

Whenever a function unit has a result ready to return to a register, it requests the CDB. When available, the CDB accepts the result and broadcasts to all reservation stations and floating-point registers both the tag of the unit supplying the result as well as the result. Any reservation station which received the tag of a function unit instead of data can then accept data available from that function unit. Any register marked *busy* also accepts data from the CDB when the register tag matches the tag of the data on the CDB.

The tag substitution process may result in floating-point registers not being involved in data transfers among the function units. In the example of loop X above, although the program specifies floating-point register 0, it will not be involved during execution of the loop. The load instruction will cancel the use of register 0. Only after the final iteration of the loop, will a value be placed in register 0 (unless another load to register 0 immediately follows the loop).

When a load instruction is encountered, it sets the busy-bit and sets the tag field of the appropriate floating-point register to indicate the assigned floating-point buffer.   Subsequent instructions, which receive data from the register, receive the tag field which indicates the floating-point buffer.   Another load, arriving before data reach the floating-point register, replaces the original tag with a pointer to the floating-point buffer participating in the current instruction sequence.

For some instruction sequences, floating-point data never reach the register specified by the program. The following example illustrates this facility of the CDB:

LD 0,A

?D 0,B   A lengthy operation

STD 0,C

LD 0,D   New sequence - clears FPR0

ADR 0,2   Finishes before lengthy op.

The second load instruction cancels the use of floating-point register 0 before data arrive.   Now independent of register 0, the register-to-register add completes before the first floating-point operation.

Floating-Point Add Unit

The floating-point add unit pipeline has three stages: (a) binary point alignment, (b) mantissa addition, and (c) normalization (Figure 4.10). The unit is fully pipelined: a floating-point addition can begin on any cycle. In combination with the reservation stations, this allows treating the adder as if there were three copies of the functional unit circuitry (i.e. as if three adders were available).

Binary Point Alignment. The characteristics (exponents) of the two operands are sent to an adder (the first in true form, the second complemented).   If the characteristics differ by more than 14, the mantissa associated with the smaller characteristic will not contribute to the sum. This permits a simplified adder to calculate only the low-order four bits of the characteristics' difference. The adder's output is forced to the maximum value of 15 and that of the difference between the characteristics. The larger characteristic becomes the characteristic of the sum and is moved to an adder for post-normalization update.

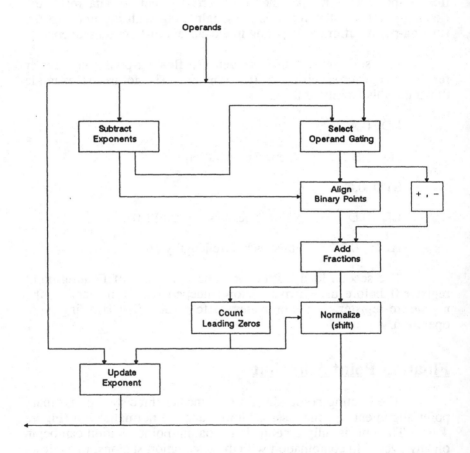

Figure 4.10 The floating-point adder

Under control of the characteristics' difference, the mantissa (fraction) associated with the smaller characteristic is gated into the shifter. The characteristics' difference is used as the shift amount. In order to minimize shift time, the shifter operates in a manner analogous to a carry lookahead adder: it gates a shift amount of 0-3 digits (based on the low-order two bits) while gating another shift of 4, 8, or 12 digits (based on the high-order two bits).

Mantissa addition. Addition of the mantissas is accomplished with a carry-lookahead adder. This approach reduces the time necessary for carries to propagate from low-order to high-order bit positions.

The carry lookahead adder is based on the observation that the sum at a particular bit position can be computed as a function of the operand bits and the prior carry, with the prior carry being independently computed.

At bit position k, the sum and carry output are given by:

$S_k = A_k$ .xor. B_k .xor. C_k

$C_k = (A_k$ .and. $B_k)$ .or. $(A_{k-1}$ .or. $B_{k-1})$ .and. C_{k-1}

A_k .and. B_k is called the carry generate term. A carry is generated into the next bit position when both operand bits are ones. A_{k-1} .or. B_{k-1} is called the carry propagate term. A carry from the prior bit position is propagated into the next bit position when either operand bit is a one.

Fan-in limitations make it impossible to implement a carry lookahead adder over the entire operand width. The implementation used in the IBM 360 model 91 treats 4-bit fields as *groups* (requiring 14 groups for the 56 bit mantissa). Two groups are combined into one *section*.

Normalization. The output of the carry lookahead adder is checked for leading zero digits (four-bit fields). The count of leading zeros is used to left shift the mantissa. At the same time, the count is subtracted from the characteristic. The left shifter is implemented in the same way as the shift unit used in the binary point alignment stage. A simplified circuit is used for the characteristic adder because the maximum shift amount is limited to 13 (and thus requires no more than four bits).

Floating-point multiply/divide Unit

A design goal for the floating-point multiply/divide unit was to allow maximum pipelining and to minimize hardware unique to either multiply or divide. It was decided to utilize a divide algorithm employing a multiplicative iteration. High speed for both multiply and divide is attained through the multiplier.

Multiply Algorithm. Binary multiplication is accomplished by adding the shifted multiplicand to the partial sum for each 1-bit in the multiplier as shown below:

```
         10101010  (multiplicand)

         10111101  (multiplier)
-------------------
-------10101010    "-": forced zero

      --------------

-----10101010--

----10101010---

---10101010----

--10101010-----

      --------------

10101010-------

111110110000010
```

The multiplier is recoded, replacing strings of one-bits (each bit requiring an addition) by strings of zero-bits (which require only one addition to the left of the string and a complemented addition to the right).

```
     10101010   (multiplicand)

     11000*01   (recoded multiplier)
-------10101010   "-": forced zero

--------------

1111101010110--   *: complement add

--------------

--------------

--------------

-10101010------

10101010-------

111110110000010
```

The multiply algorithm of the IBM 360 model 91 is based on multiplier recoding, but does not require the variable shifts associated with that method. Instead, recoding is accomplished using successive 3-bit fields which overlap a single bit. The overlap allows a string of ones of length greater than 2 to be recoded as a single string of zeros.

In one iteration, six fields are recoded and the appropriate partial products are added. Five iterations are required to recode the entire multiplier. Figure 4.11 illustrates the recoding and partial product iterations.

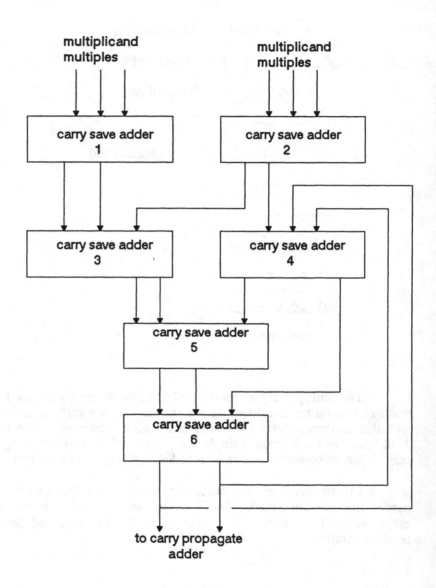

Figure 4.11 The floating-point multiplier

A carry-save adder tree is used to hide the carry ripple time of each of the intermediate partial product additions. The carry-save adder operates on a sequence of additions by treating the carry output of one iteration (shifted one position to the left) as an input to the next iteration. A carry-propagate adder is used for the final iteration as there are no further opportunities to accommodate carries generated at that time.

Divide Algorithm. Standard algorithms for division were not considered for implementation as their speed was not commensurate with that attained by the multiply algorithm. The availability of a high speed multiplier provided an impetus to design a divide algorithm based upon multiplication. The resulting design utilizes the multiplier unit hardware in an iterative algorithm with rapid (quadratic) convergence.

The difference in algorithm results in a minor incompatibility with other machines in the IBM 360 family. The low-order bit of the quotient produced by the IBM 360 model 91 may differ from that produced by the rest of the IBM 360 family. The remainder produced by a divide operation (assuming a positive dividend and positive divisor) on the model 91 has magnitude less than or equal to half the divisor. Other models produce a positive remainder between zero and the divisor. Numerically, the result produced on the model 91 is superior. When the remainder is zero, the model 91 results are the same as those produced by other models.

Floating-point division is performed by a sequence of multiplications. The sequence of multipliers is chosen so that it drives the divisor toward one, with quadratic convergence (i.e. the number of bits of precision of the product doubles with each iteration). Each time the divisor is multiplied, the dividend is multiplied by the same value. The dividend and divisor may be thought of as the numerator and denominator of a fraction (the quotient). As the denominator is driven to one, the dividend is driven to the quotient value. In the example below, A and B are the mantissa of the dividend and divisor, respectively. To divide A by B, perform the following sequence of multiplications:

$$(A/B) (M_0/M_0) (M_1/M_1) (M_2/M_2) \cdots (M_n/M_n) = (Q/1)$$

The choice of the M_i is constrained by the requirement that they be easily determined (i.e. that a modest amount of hardware will suffice).   A goal in the selection of the M_i is to attain rapid convergence in order to minimize the number of iterations required.

In normalized form,

$.5 \leq B < 1,$

where B is the mantissa of the divisor. Thus, B can be written as:

$B = 1 - b, \text{ where } b < .5 .$

Recalling that:

$(1 - b) (1 + b) = 1 - b^2 ,$

leads to choosing

$M_0 = 1 + b,$

the 2's complement of the divisor,

$1 - b .$

This results in

$(B) (M_0) = 1 - b^2 .$

Similarly,

$(1 - b^2) (1 + b^2) = 1 - b^4 ,$

and,

$M_1 = 1 + b^2,$

the two's complement of the divisor's current value. For the kth iteration

$(1 - b^{2 \exp k}) (1 + b^{2 \exp k}) = 1 - b^{2 \exp k + 1} ,$

resulting in

$$M_k = 1 + b\,2\exp k,$$

the two's complement of the divisor's current value,

$$1 - b\,2\exp k = (B)\,(M_1)\,(M_2) \cdots (M_{k-1}).$$

Since,

$$b < .5,$$

$1-b\,2\exp k$ converges quadratically to 1. This means that the number of bits of precision in the divisor (when considered as an approximation to 1) doubles with each iteration. With B normalized, the mantissa's high-order bit is a one-bit, guaranteeing an initial precision of at least one correct bit. The number of leading one-bits doubles after each iteration to 2, 4, 8, 16, 32, and 64 bits. After six iterations, full precision floating-point accuracy is attained.   (Of course, the final multiply of the divisor is not necessary. It would result in the value one for the denominator, leaving the quotient in the numerator.)

A further improvement can be made by substituting a table-lookup for the first three multiplies. The table-lookup provides the value of the first multiplier and assures that the product will be precise to seven bits. The second product will be precise to 14 bits; the third will be precise to 28 bits; the fourth will be precise to 56 bits.

The multipliers may be truncated in order to improve performance, since full precision products are not needed. Additionally, the multiplications of numerator and denominator are performed concurrently in alternate stages of the pipeline as illustrated in Figure 4.12.

STORAGE SYSTEM

With its aggressive clock cycle (60 nanoseconds), highly concurrent mode of instruction processing, and expectations for large input/output configurations, the IBM 360 model 91 storage system must provide high capacity, high peak performance, and high typical performance. These high levels of performance are obtained by using a three-level storage system.

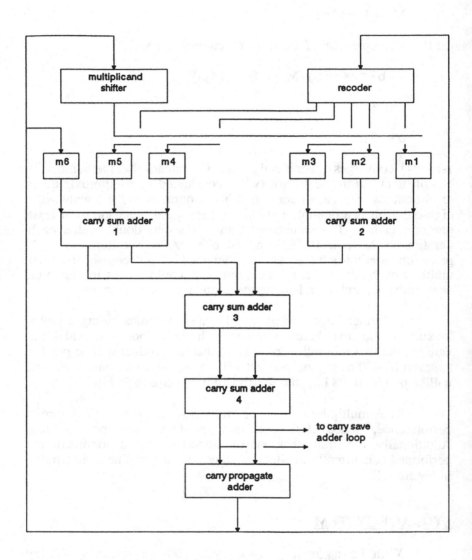

Figure 4.12 The floating-point divider

The first level is *main storage*, available either as 1 megabyte
(2^{20}) with 8-way interleave or as 2 megabytes with 16-way interleave.
In each case, the effective cycle time is 780 nanoseconds, with an

access time of 600 nanoseconds. The storage unit's internal cycle time of 750 nanoseconds is not achievable as the cycle time must be a multiple of the processor's 60 nanosecond clock ($780 = 13 * 60$). The *main storage control element* (MSCE) is responsible for handling all accesses to main storage.

The second level consists of *extended main storage*, available as either 2 or 4 megabytes, with a 780 nanosecond cycle time, but with an access time of 900 nanoseconds. The access time is greater than the cycle time because the extended main storage is located a long distance from the central processor. The *peripheral storage control element* (PSCE) is responsible for handling all accesses to extended main storage.

The third level is the input/output system, including peripheral equipment. Although architecturally common with the rest of the IBM 360 family, the input/output system is implemented as part of the PSCE.

Although they differ in timing, the main storage and extended main storage are functionally identical. Instructions, processor data, and input/output data can reside in either memory. To minimize the impact of the difference in speed, a *storage channel* is provided. Operating as an input/output device (although actually part of the PSCE), the storage channel can transfer data between main storage and extended main storage concurrently with program execution as well as other input/output activities.

With the exception of main storage, the two machines designated the model 95 are identical to the models 91. In the model 95, magnetic thin-film memory is used in place of 780 nanosecond core storage. The cycle time of the thin film memory is 120 nanoseconds, with a 180 nanosecond access time.

Main Storage Control Element

All central processor storage accesses are handled through the MSCE. Those accesses which are addressed to extended main storage are sent to the PSCE for handling. The MSCE:

1. Buffers stores and fetches when storage is busy;

2. Retains sequential ordering of multiple stores and fetches to the same address;

3. Optimizes the case of a fetch which follows a store to the same address; and

4. Optimizes multiple fetches to the same address.

Figure 4.13 shows the logical structure of the MSCE. The MSCE contains:

1 Three store data buffers (SDB);

2. Three store address registers (SAR);

3. A five position accept stack;

4. A four position request stack; and

5. A storage address bus.

The three store data buffers and their corresponding store address registers are implemented in the MSCE, although they are conceptually part of the floating-point execution unit. The store address registers and store data buffers hold storage addresses and data to be stored. Only the floating-point store instructions, STD or STE, cause data to be stored.

Handling of Fetch Requests. A fetch request originating within the central processor is sent to the MSCE. If the addressed storage module is busy, the request is allowed to issue if the MSCE has an available slot in the request stack. If the request is for a main storage access, it is sent to the addressed module and to the accept stack. If the request is for extended main storage, it is sent to the PSCE. At the conclusion of the storage access, the fetched data are sent to the appropriate data or instruction buffer.

If the main storage module or the PSCE is busy, the request cannot be accepted. Instead, it is sent to the *request stack* (which is actually a first-in-first-out queue). At the conclusion of the main storage module or PSCE busy condition, the first item in the request stack is re-initiated, as if it was just received from the central processor.

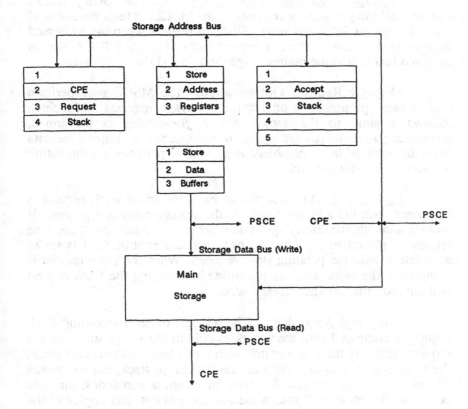

Figure 4.13 The main storage control element

Handling of Store Requests. A store request originating within the central processor is sent to the MSCE. The request is issued only if one of the storage address registers is available. If so, the store address and data are placed in a free storage address register and its corresponding storage data buffer. In a manner analogous to the treatment of fetches, the storage request is sent to the addressed main storage module and the accept stack, or to the PSCE. If busy, the storage request is placed, instead, in the request stack. When the main storage module or PSCE is no longer busy, the first request of the request stack is initiated as above.

Fetch/Store Requests From The PSCE. The PSCE performs its own buffering of storage requests to the MSCE. It tests the status of main storage modules and only initiates a request when the addressed main storage module is free. A request initiated by the PSCE is always accepted and sent to the main storage module and the accept stack.

Multiple Request Optimization. The MSCE may perform one of two optimizations on incoming storage requests. If a fetch follows a store to the same address, *forwarding* is performed, eliminating a second storage cycle. If multiple fetches request the data from the same address, *combined accessing* is performed, eliminating all but the first storage cycle.

Forwarding. The address of each incoming fetch request is compared with the addresses held in the storage address registers. If there is a match, the fetch request does not initiate a storage cycle. The request is placed in the request stack, and the control field is set to associate it with the pending store request. When the store request is completed, the store data are transmitted, satisfying the fetch request without requiring another storage access.

Combined Accessing. The address of each incoming fetch request is compared with the addresses held in the accept stack and the request stack. If there is a match with an address in the accept stack, the incoming fetch is also entered into the accept stack, but no storage access is initiated. When the cycle in progress concludes, multiple accept stack entries will match the storage address, and copies of the data are returned to requesters, thereby requiring only one storage access.

If there is a match with an address in the request stack, the address is placed into the accept stack with control information which will cause only one storage access cycle.

Peripheral Storage Control Element

The Peripheral Storage Control Element handles all storage requests addressed to extended main storage; controls input/output activities; and manages the storage channel. The PSCE is comprised of the bus control, common channel control, and the storage channel.

Bus Control. The bus control contains a request stack (more properly termed a register file) for accesses to extended main storage. If a storage access request addresses a module of extended main storage which is busy, the data address (and data for a store) is placed in the request stack. When a storage module completes a cycle and becomes available, the request stack is checked for any access requiring the module. If a match is found, the access is begun.

Common Channel Control. The common channel control provides an interface between the IBM 360 model 91 processor/storage complex and the standard IBM 360 channels. Consistent with the model 91 philosophy, it initiates fetch request for high speed input/output devices in advance of requirement to reduce the probability of an overrun.

Storage Channel. From an architectural perspective, the storage channel appears to be an input/output facility. It is implemented within the PSCE, and its function is the transmission of blocks of data between main storage and extended main storage. The implementation outboard of the central processor allows the storage channel to operate concurrently with other processor and input/output activities. With no memory interference, the peak transfer rate is 66 megabytes per second.

A central processor *start input/output* instruction transmits a channel program to the storage channel. The channel program indicates the fetch address, store address, size of the data block to be transferred, and the direction of the transfer (main storage to extended main storage or the reverse). Gather and scatter operations are available.

The storage channel uses the bus control located within the PSCE. Special tagging of storage channel operations allows effective exploitation of the request stack. Fetch requests are placed in the request stack with their corresponding store addresses held in the associated data fields of the request stack. As fetches are initiated, the store address replaces the no longer needed fetch address in the request stack. When the storage cycle completes, the fetched data are stored in

the (now available) data field of the initiating request stack entry.
Then, store requests are processed normally.

CHAPTER 5

THE CDC STAR-100

PERSPECTIVE

In 1970, Control Data Corporation announced the STAR-100 (STring ARray), a large-scale computer with a new, vector architecture. The STAR-100 was designed to solve large computational problems in science and engineering

The STAR-100 possessed a powerful computational unit focused on arithmetic (floating point) and logical (boolean) operations. Boolean operations could be performed on bit or byte operands. The basic floating-point word-size was 64 bits. Computations on 32-bit words were performed at least twice as fast. The floating-point processing rates are shown in Table 5.1.

OPERATION	RATE (OP'N/SEC.)
32-bit add, subtract	100,000,000
32-bit multiply	100,000,000
32-bit divide	50,000,000
32-bit square root	50,000,000
64-bit add, subtract	50,000,000
64-bit multiply	25,000,000
64-bit divide	12,500,000
65-bit square root	12,500,000

Table 5.1 Floating-Point Speeds

The STAR-100 was designed for rapid processing of vectors, and featured pipelined functional units. These same functional units were also used for scalar operations. This new architecture offered high peak speed for those programs with highly structured data. Such programs were able to exploit the vector processing capabilities of the STAR. When the data were not highly structured, the STAR did not perform well. With scalar operands, the use of a pipelined functional unit increased delay and limited performance.

Performance of the STAR was highly dependent on successfully structuring a program as a sequence of (long) vector operations. A speed ratio of 10:1 was not unusual for different versions of a program. In contrast, the performance of earlier machines was relatively independent of program style. A rule of thumb for estimating running time was to form the weighted sum of the number of floating-point additions and the number of floating-point multiplications. In the case of the IBM 7090, which had little overlap, this technique was generally accurate to within 30 per cent. For the CDC 6600 and IBM 360/91, which had extensive instruction overlap, the variation between similar programs could be a factor of three or two, respectively. Special compilers, developed for each of these machines, included an optimizing pass which reordered instructions for maximum speed.

The STAR-100 included virtual memory, a capability generally associated with programming convenience but not with high performance. CDC designers believed that, in the context of vector operations of hundreds or thousands of elements, program locality was sufficiently high so that virtual memory would not incur a large performance penalty. These designers were also working in the context of IBM's newly announced System/370 featuring virtual memory.

ARCHITECTURE

The STAR computer (Figure 5.1) consists of:

1. A storage access control supervising all transfers of data to or from magnetic-core storage;

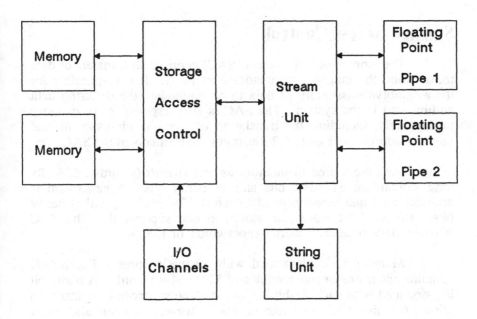

Figure 5.1 The STAR 100 Central Processor

2. A stream unit responsible for supplying operands to the floating-point pipeline and returning results to storage;

3. A string unit performing operations on variable-length byte strings;

4. A floating-point unit performing arithmetic on vector operands; and

5. A magnetic-core storage memory holding program and data and providing vector operands at the rate required by the stream unit or string unit.

Vector operations are performed by three-address instructions which fetch operands from storage, calculate results, and transmit them to storage. The instruction set is based upon APL [IVE62] and offers the facilities found in that language. A register file is present for address calculations and scalar operations.

Storage Access Control

The storage access control (SAC) controls all transfers of data to, or from, the magnetic-core storage memory. It is responsible for the assembly/disassembly of data to accommodate the differing data widths used in the system. The SAC is also responsible for memory management, including the translation of virtual addresses to real memory addresses. Figure 5.2 illustrates the elements of the SAC.

Data are stored in memory as *superwords* (swords), 528 bits long, containing 512 data bits and 16 parity bits. A superword is arranged as 4 quarter-superwords; each is 128 bits long with 4 parity bits. Eight 64-bit words are stored in one superword. The SAC transfers data in units of quarter-superwords, or 128 bits.

Memory is implemented with magnetic cores. The STAR contains either one or two modules of 512K 64-bit words. A parity bit is associated with each 32-bit half-word. The superword organization allows the high streaming rate necessary for vector operands. Only minor complexity is introduced by the need to accommodate a smaller data width for other operations.

The STAR processes floating-point data in either 32-bit format (half word) or 64-bit format (word). Write operations are flagged to indicate which 32 bit portions of a sword will be modified. Input/output channels accept and provide data in 16-bit units.

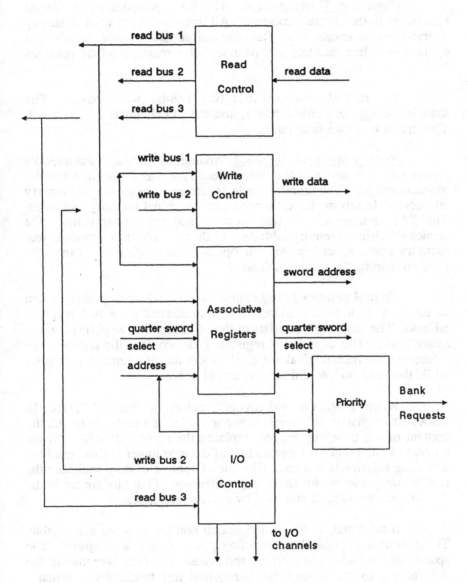

Figure 5.2 Storage Access Control

Read and Write Access. The SAC provides three 128-bit read buses to the central processor. All three buses are used to supply operands to the stream unit. Data for instructions and for input/output operations utilize read bus 3. The associative registers utilize read bus 1.

The central processor has two 128-bit write buses. The associative registers utilize bus 1, and the I/O channels utilize bus 2. The stream unit uses both buses.

Virtual memory access. Analogous to the System/360's supervisor state and problem state, the STAR has 2 program modes: monitor and job. The monitor mode generates accesses to real memory addresses. In job mode, all accesses are to virtual memory addresses. The SAC determines the real memory address corresponding to a requested virtual memory address. If there is no corresponding real memory address, an input/output operation is performed to read the page containing the virtual address.

Virtual address translation. In job mode, every address sent to the SAC is a virtual address and is translated to a real memory address. The *page table* consists of the 16 *associative registers* and the *space table*. The associative registers (AR) contain the last 16 page references in chronological order. The most recent reference is in AR_0, while the 16th most recent reference is in AR_{15}.

When a virtual address is received in the SAC, the 16 associative registers are searched in one cycle. If a match is found, the content of the matching register replaces the content of AR_0, and the content of each register replaces that of the next lower register until the matching register is reached. The (new) content of AR_0 indicates the real memory address for the storage reference. Flag bits are set in the AR whenever a page is modified by a write reference.

If no match is found, the search continues in the space table. These entries contain the remaining pages within a program. The space table is located in storage, and access to it is slower than to the AR (access to the space table is required less frequently). When a match is found in the space table, the same entry reorganization occurs as does with the AR. Here, it is possible that the page is not in real memory, and the monitor must be notified to fetch the page.

Input/Output Channels. The twelve input/output (I/O) channels are implemented as part of the storage access control. Data are transmitted between the I/O channels and the memory as quarter-swords, 128-bits. An assembly/disassembly register, shared among all the channels, serves as the buffer between the memory access buses (128 bits) and each channel's assembly/disassembly register (32 bits). The assembly/disassembly register utilizes a 16-bit path to peripheral stations.

When there is a memory access conflict, I/O channels receive the lowest priority. The large amount of buffering provided in the SAC assembly/disassembly register and the channels' assembly/disassembly registers minimizes the probability of an overrun condition.

In case of multiple requests for storage access among the channels, channel 1 has the highest priority, and each higher numbered channel has successively lower priority. When a high priority channel is blocked due to a memory busy condition, it reissues its request only on alternate cycles. This leaves every other cycle available for other channels to initiate memory accesses, while the first channel's request remains pending.

Stream Unit

The stream unit (Figure 5.3) is responsible for accessing data from storage; operating on data, or providing data to the floating-point pipeline; and returning results to storage. Execution of a vector instruction typically requires many (dozens to thousands) cycles, during which time the instruction processor prepares for the next instruction's execution. A 32-word instruction stack buffers instructions and decreases the number of memory accesses required. Due to the vector orientation of the system, the instruction processing mechanism did not receive emphasis during design.

The functions of the stream unit are: (a) storage access, (b) address operations, (c) operations on strings, and (d) instruction processing.

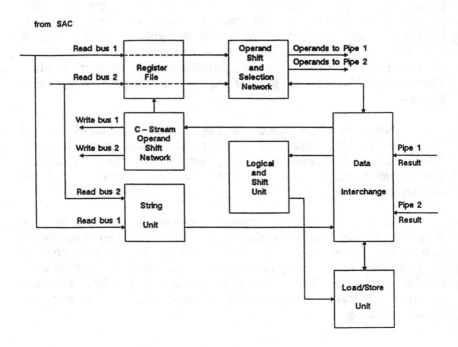

Figure 5.3 The Stream Unit

Storage Access. There are two data paths available for receiving operands from memory via the storage access control. A third data path sends results to memory via the storage access control. A 1024-byte buffer (16 swords) holds input data, which may be received faster than they can be used in certain string operations. The buffer, working with the operand shift networks, provides a place where operand alignment can be performed when needed. Operands are sent to the floating-point pipes as pairs, even though they may arrive in the stream unit at different times.

Address operations. The stream unit contains a *register file* which holds index values, operand and result addresses, and operation lengths. Some instructions are available to manipulate data within the register file. The register file is seen by the programmer as a set of 256 registers of 64 bits. It is organized as an array of 128 quarter swords (128-bits) to maximize the data transfer rate to, and from, memory.

String operations. The string unit is described in detail in the next section. Its operands are strings of data. The string unit performs: (a) arithmetic operations, (b) decimal edit operations, and (c) logical operations.

Instruction processing. An instruction stack, illustrated in Figure 5.4, decouples instruction availability from storage access time. The stack holds 4 swords, in cyclic fashion, stored by the low order bits of the sword address. When an instruction is issued, the next sword is requested if it is not already in the stack. Branches to instructions in the stack (those instructions in the same sword, in the next sword, or in the prior two swords) do not require a storage access. Branches to instructions outside the instruction stack clear the stack and initiate an instruction fetch.

String Unit

Arithmetic operations. The string unit performs arithmetic operations (add, subtract, multiply, divide, and compare) on variable-length byte strings. Binary operations are performed on bit-fields of specified length. Decimal operations are carried out on byte fields containing packed decimal values (two decimal digits per byte).

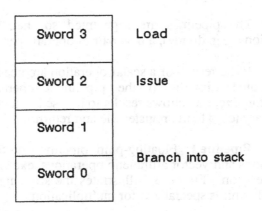

Figure 5.4 Instruction Stack

Decimal edit operations. These operations manipulate string data but do not perform arithmetic. Shifts, merges, and comparisons are among the operations performed. The format of data may be changed, or a byte-by-byte comparison may be performed.

Logical operations. Logical, or boolean, operations are performed on variable length byte strings. The following operations may be specified: (a) and, (b) equivalence, (c) exclusive or, (d) implication, (e) inhibit, (f) nand, (g) nor, and (h) or.

Flag bits are set at the conclusion of a logical operation, indicating whether the result bits are all zeros, all ones, or a mixture of zeros and ones.

Floating-Point Unit

The floating-point unit contains two distinct pipelines. Each pipeline performs floating-point vector arithmetic. Where an operation is performed by each pipeline, the vector operands are divided so that odd numbered elements are sent to pipeline 1, and even numbered elements are sent to pipeline 2.

Floating-point arithmetic is available for either 64-bit words or 32-bit words. In 32-bit mode, the (64-bit wide) pipelines simultaneously process a pair of 32-bit words.. The speed of 32-bit mode is at least twice that of 64-bit mode.

The pipelines are segmented so that, except for iterative operations (e.g. divide), a new pair of operands enters them each cycle.

If the results of a scalar operation are needed as operands, they are routed directly to the pipeline's operand input. Called *shortstopping*, this allows results to be used without incurring the time necessary to go to the register file and return.

Pipeline 1. Floating-point pipeline 1 performs address register operations and vector arithmetic operations, except division and square root iteration. Figure 5.5 illustrates the structure of pipeline 1. The multiply unit is specialized for multiplication.

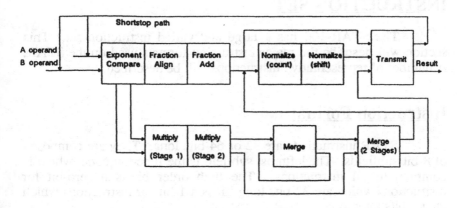

Figure 5.5 Pipeline 1

Pipeline 2. Floating-point pipeline 2 performs address addition/subtraction and all vector arithmetic operations, including division and square root iteration. Figure 5.6 illustrates the structure of pipeline 2. The multipurpose unit performs the vector operations of division, multiplication, and square root iteration. It has far more circuit elements than the multiply unit of pipeline 1. The low occurrence of division and square root iteration did not justify the expense of a multipurpose unit in each pipeline. There is a separate divide unit for register arithmetic.

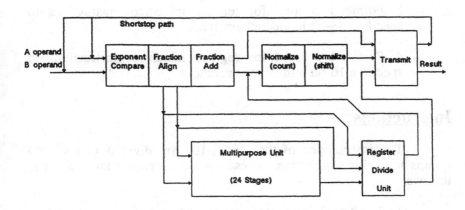

Figure 5.6 Pipeline 2

INSTRUCTION SET

The STAR-100 has a large and varied instruction set. This section will describe the major instruction formats used on the STAR. A number of representative instructions will be described.

Instruction Format

STAR instructions are 32 or 64 bits long. They are composed of 8-bit subfields. The leftmost subfield is the function code, which is common to all instructions. The high order bit is a zero-bit for instructions which are 32 bits long. It is a 1-bit for instructions which are 64 bits long.

A number of different instruction formats are used, as illustrated in Figure 5.7 and described below.

1. Format 1 is used by vector instructions and by string instructions to specify two input operand storage addresses and an output operand storage address. Format 1 is also used by some branch instructions to specify their operands.

2. Format 2 is used for register instructions to specify two input registers and an output register. Format 2 is also used by some branch instructions to specify their operands.

3. Format 3 is used for register increment instructions to specify a 48-bit immediate operand.

4. Format 4 is used for register increment instructions to specify a 16-bit immediate operand.

Instructions

The instructions of the STAR-100 are divided into several groups according to function. These instruction groups are defined as follows:

1. The branch instructions control program flow.

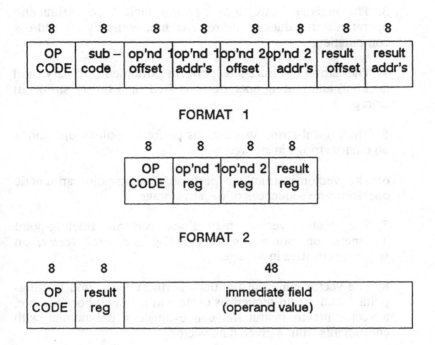

FORMAT 1

FORMAT 2

FORMAT 3

FORMAT 4

Figure 5.7 Instruction Format

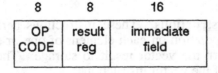

2. The index instructions increment index registers and control loop iterations.

3. The register instructions perform logical and arithmetic operations on values in the register file, primarily for address computation.

4. The string instructions perform arithmetic (binary and decimal) and editing operations on BCD and binary strings in storage.

5. The logical-string instructions perform boolean operations on binary strings in storage.

6. The vector instructions perform floating-point arithmetic operations on sequences of data in storage.

7. The sparse vector instructions perform floating-point arithmetic operations, as directed by a *control vector*, on sequences of data in storage.

8. The vector macro instructions perform compound floating-point functions on sequences of data in storage. For example, a vector macro instruction can evaluate a polynomial with coefficients from a given data vector.

9. A number of other instructions are provided to carry out specialized functions. An example of an instruction in this group is one which reads the interval timer.

Vector instructions. These instructions perform a floating-point arithmetic operation on each element of one or two vector input operands and return the vector result to storage. The following is a brief description of the vector instructions:

1. Addition. The elements of the two input vectors are added and their sums are stored. The additions produce double precision results. An instruction modifier selects either the high-order (upper) part or the low-order (lower) part of the sum. If the high-order part is selected, it may optionally be normalized.

2. Subtraction. The elements of the second input vector are subtracted from those of the first input vector, and their differences are stored. The same options are available for

selection of the upper or lower results, with optional normalization of the upper results.

3. Multiplication. The elements of the two input vectors are multiplied, and their products are stored. Either the upper or lower products are selected. Normalization is not an option. The significance option, available for multiply and divide, ensures that each result has a significance count no greater than the significance count of either of its operands. If necessary, the results are right shifted to decrease their significance counts.

4. Division. The elements of the second input vector are divided by those of the first input vector, and their quotients are stored. In significance mode, the results are right shifted until the significance counts are no greater than the significance counts of either of the two input operands.

5. Square root. The square roots of the elements of the input vector are stored. The significance counts of the results are no greater than the significance counts of the input operands.

6. Address addition/subtraction. The rightmost 48 bits of the elements of two input vectors are added/subtracted and their sums/differences are stored. The 48 bit fields are treated as unsigned integers. Overflows are ignored as they are equivalent to address wraparound.

7. Transmit and modify. The input vector elements are transmitted to the output vector. Before transmission, one of the following unary operations is performed: (a) floor, the greatest integer less than or equal to the operand; (b) ceiling, the smallest integer greater than or equal to the operand; (c) mask exponent, the integer value of the exponent portion of the operand; (d) truncate, the closest integer with magnitude less than or equal to the operand; (e) absolute value, the operand with its sign forced positive; (f) extend the 64-bit value obtained by affixing low-order zeros to the 32-bit operand; (g) contract, the 32-bit value obtained by discarding the low-order part of the 64-bit operand; and (h) rounded contract, the 32-bit value obtained by discarding the low order part of the 64-bit operand after rounding at bit 32.

8. Combine. The elements of the two input operands are combined and stored. One of the following operations specifies how the data are combined: (a) pack, the exponent of the first operand and the coefficient of the second operand are combined; (b) unnormalize, the first operand's coefficient is shifted while the first element's exponent is simultaneously adjusted until it equals the second operand's exponent; or (c) adjust significance, the coefficient of the first operand is shifted while its exponent is simultaneously adjusted by the integer value of the second operand

Sparse vector instructions. These instructions are used when the elements of a vector are predominantly zero. Their use allows conservation of both space and time. Sparse vectors store the nonzero values contiguously. An associated bit-vector, the *order vector*, contains a one-bit for every nonzero element and a zero-bit for every zero element in the sparse vector.

A compress instruction creates a sparse vector and associated order vector from a conventional vector. There are two forms of the compress instruction:

1. An existing order vector selects elements from a conventional vector. These elements are placed in consecutive storage locations, creating a sparse vector. This technique is used to create sparse vectors with known structural properties.

2. A conventional vector, the sparse vector's source, is compared with a second conventional vector, the threshhold vector. The sparse vector is formed from all the elements in the conventional vector which are greater than their corresponding threshhold element. The order vector is created at the same time.

The length of a sparse vector operation is controlled by the result vector's length field. The stream unit supplies zero for an operand if the corresponding bit of the operand's associated order vector is zero or if the operation has continued beyond the length of an input vector. For each result stored, the corresponding order vector bit is set.

The following operations are available in sparse vector format:

1. Addition. When the input operands' order vectors indicate that at least one of the two input operands is nonzero, they are added; their sum is stored in the output vector; and the corresponding bit of the order vector is set. The additions produce double precision results. An instruction modifier selects either the high-order (upper) part or the low-order (lower) part of the sum. If the high-order part is selected, it may be normalized (an option).

2. Subtraction. When the input operands' order vectors indicate that at least one of the two input operands is nonzero, they are subtracted; their difference is stored in the output vector; and the corresponding bit of the order vector is set. Either upper or lower result may be selected, with optional normalization of the upper result.

3. Multiplication. When the input operands' order vectors indicate that the two input operands are nonzero, they are multiplied; their product is stored in the output vector; and the corresponding bit of the order vector is set. Either the upper or lower products are selected. Normalization is not an option. The significance option, available for sparse vector multiply and divide, ensures that the result has a significance count no greater than the significance count of either of its operands. If necessary, the result is right shifted to decrease its significance count.

4. Division. When the input operands' order vectors indicate that the two input operands are nonzero, they are divided; their quotient is stored in the output vector; and the corresponding bit of the order vector is set. In significance mode, the result is right shifted until the significance counts are no greater than the significance counts of either of the two input operands.

Vector macro instructions. A vector macro instruction replaces a sequence of instructions needed for compound operations. The use of internal registers, which are not available to programmers, allows vector macro instructions to attain speeds not otherwise possible. When the order of arithmetic operations within a vector macro operation is changed from the usual order to improve performance, that is noted. Several of the most important vector macro instructions are:

1. Sum reduction, $(+/ A_i)$. The input vector, A, is fetched by the stream unit. Odd-numbered elements are transmitted to floating-point pipeline 1, and even-numbered elements are transmitted to floating-point pipeline 2. A partial sum is accumulated by each pipeline as the elements are processed. At the conclusion of the input vector, the two partial sums are added to produce the final sum.

2. Product reduction, $(*/ A_i)$. This vector macro instruction is similar to the sum reduction operation above, with addition replaced by multiplication.

3. Dot product, $(+/ A_i B_i)$. The input vectors, A and B, are fetched by the stream unit. Odd-numbered elements are transmitted to floating-point pipeline 1, and even-numbered elements are transmitted to floating-point pipeline 2. Each pipeline forms the product of the operands and returns it to the floating-point adder where a partial sum is accumulated. At the conclusion of the input vector, the two partial sums are added to produce the final sum.

4. Average sum, $(C_i = \{A_i + B_i\} / 2)$. Corresponding elements of the input operands are averaged, and the result is stored.

5. Average difference, $(C_i = \{A_i - B_i\} / 2)$. This vector macro operation is similar to the average sum above, with addition replaced by subtraction.

6. Delta, $(C_i = A_{i+1} - A_i)$. The difference of a pair of consecutive elements is stored.

7. Adjacent mean, $(C_i = \{A_i + A_{i+1}\} / 2)$. The average of a pair of consecutive elements is stored.

8. Gather, $(C[i] = B[A[i]])$, where [] represents a subscript operation. This vector macro operation, called *transmit indexed list* by CDC, brings scattered data into contiguous storage locations. The integer values A_i are used to select the elements of B which are stored in C_i. This operation is analogous to indirect addressing at the hardware level or, within a programming language, to two levels of subscripting.

9. Scatter, $(C[B[i]] = A[i])$.   This vector macro operation, called *transmit list to indexed result* by CDC, is the inverse of the gather instruction noted above.

10. Polynomial Evaluation, $(C_i = P_B(A_i))$, where

$$P_B(x) = B_n + B_{n-1}x + \dots B_1 x^{n-1} + B_0 x^n .$$

This vector macro operation constructs the polynomial, P_B, with coefficients from input vector B, and evaluates it for each element of input vector A. The results are stored in C.

CHAPTER 6

THE ILLIAC IV

PERSPECTIVE

The ILLIAC IV was an experimental machine, produced by Burroughs Corporation under contract to the University of Illinois. Funding for the development of the system came from the Advanced Research Projects Agency, DoD. The original goal of the project was to produce a machine which had a speed of 10^9 floating-point operations per second. To achieve this goal, a system with 256 parallel processing elements was planned. Due to technological problems and consequent cost growth, the ILLIAC IV was built with 64 processing elements and attained a speed of $1.6 \cdot 10^8$ floating-point operations per second.

The structure of the ILLIAC IV is based on a number of economic and technical advantages:

1. The design cost of a general-purpose computer scales with size (number of components). The use of 64 identical processing elements permitted a smaller design effort than is ordinarily associated with a machine of this size.

2. The task of designing a conventional high speed computer becomes increasingly more difficult as the computer's size and speed increase. Since the speed of electricity is finite, circuits requiring communication with one another within one clock cycle, must be physically close. Parallel operation, as implemented in the ILLIAC IV, minimizes the number of circuits constrained by these limitations.

3. A large number of physical problems map directly onto the structure of the ILLIAC IV. Problems involving large matrices, image processing, and systems of partial differential equations, such as those of meteorology, aeronautics, and nuclear engineering are well suited to the ILLIAC IV.

ARCHITECTURE

The ILLIAC IV array consists of a *control unit* and an *array processor*. The control unit (CU) performs scalar operations, address computations, loop control, and generation of microinstruction sequences for the array processor. Parallel arithmetic and logical operations are performed by the array processor. The array processor is an 8x8 array of 64 identical processing elements (PEs). The PEs are numbered from 0 to 63, going left to right within a row, starting at the upper left corner. Each PE routes data to its four nearest neighbors: (a) the PEs on the right and on the left (+1 and -1) and (b) the PEs above and below(+8 and -8). Associated with each PE is a processing element memory (PEM), with a storage capacity of 2048 words of 64 bits.

The Control Unit

The control unit carries out all processing functions which are not accomplished by the array processor. These include (a) operating system functions, (b) address and index generation, (c) loop control, and (d) generation of microinstruction sequences to control the processing elements. The CU is comprised of five major elements (Figure 6.1) which operate concurrently: (a) register file, (b) instruction look-ahead unit, (c) advanced station, (d) final station, and (e) memory service unit.

Control unit organization. Instructions enter the CU at the instruction look-ahead and are sent, in turn, to the advanced station and the final station. Instructions performing housekeeping functions are executed only at the advanced station unit. Instructions specifying PE operations are placed on the *final station queue.* The final station queue allows the advanced station and final station to operate independently, at varying rates, and usually without delaying one another. When instructions reach the final station unit, their execution results in generation of control sequences for the PE array.

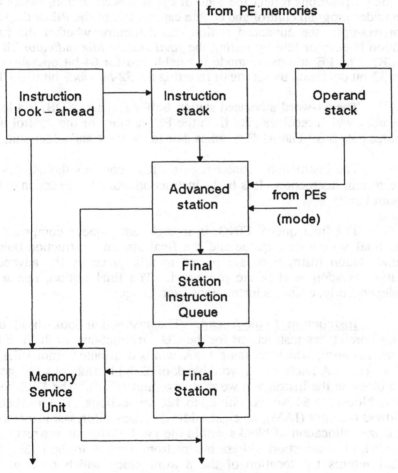

Figure 6.1 Control unit block diagram

Registers. The major control unit registers are given below.

The four advanced station accumulator registers, AC_0, AC_1, AC_2, and AC_3, are 64-bit general purpose registers. They receive data from the control unit result data bus, the PE array, or PE memory. These registers send data to the control unit source data bus, the logic and adder units, and the advanced station instruction register.

The advanced station control register, ACR, is 16 bits long. Some bit positions reflect the state of the advanced station; others are set under program control and enable capabilities of the PE or the CU. For example, the advanced station can determine whether the final station is busy or idle by testing the *final station idle indicator* bit of ACR. The PE arithmetic mode is established for 64-bit operation or for 32-bit operation by setting or resetting the *32-bit mode* bit of ACR.

The 64-word advanced station buffer register, ADB, is a local memory which receives data from the PE memory or the control unit source data bus. The ADB supplies data to the logic and adder units.

The instruction counter register, ICR, contains the address of the current instruction. It is in the instruction look-ahead section of the control unit.

The final queue, FINQ, is an eight entry queue comprised of the final station data queue and the final station instruction queue. Final station instructions are placed in this queue by the advanced station as soon as they are processed. The final station, operating independently, executes instructions from the queue.

Instruction Look-Ahead. The instruction look-ahead unit (ILA) prefetches instructions for the CU. Instructions are held in the array memory, which contains 128K words distributed among the 64 PEs. The ILA fetches an 8-word block of 32-bit instructions and stores the block in the instruction word storage unit (IWS). The IWS holds eight blocks, or 64 words, with up to 128 instructions. The instruction address memory (IAM), an eight-address content-addressable memory, manages allocation of blocks within the IWS. When an instruction is needed, the instruction address is sent from the ILA to the IAM. The IAM returns the location of the 8-word block which contains the instruction within the IWS (Figure 6.2). The ILA selects the required instruction word from within the block.

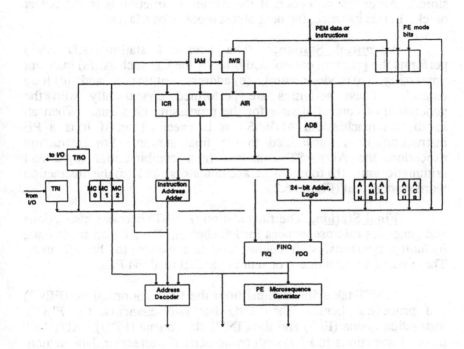

Figure 6.2 Control unit registers

The ILA fetches a new block of instructions for the IWS under one or more of the following conditions:

1. The current instruction is in the last half of a block (one of the last eight instructions of a block), and the next block is not in the IWS.

2. The current instruction is a branch, and a new instruction stream is about to begin.

3. An interrupt changes the instruction counter.

The IWS attempts to retain the instruction blocks most likely to be needed. A circular counter is used to keep track of the order in which blocks are stored. Ordinarily, the oldest instruction block, the one lowest in the counter, is overlaid when a new instruction block is stored. An exception occurs if the current instruction is in the oldest block. In this instance, the next oldest block is overlayed.

Advanced Station. The advanced station (ADVAST) performs the program control activities of the CU such as: (a) interrupt processing, (b) mode control, (c) address arithmetic, and (d) loop control. These activities are performed concurrently with the generation of control signals for the processing elements. When an instruction reaches the ADVAST it is executed or, if it is a PE instruction, it is transmitted to the final station. For instruction execution, the ADVAST contains: (a) a combinatorial logic and arithmetic unit, (b) four 64-bit accumulators, and (c) the instruction word storage unit (Figure 6.2).

Final Station. The final station (FINST) decodes instructions and generates microsequences for PE control. FINST also sends data, including operands, shift counts, and test values, to the PE array. These items are *broadcast*, or sent in parallel to all 64 PEs.

FINST takes instructions from the final station queue (FINQ) and processes them. The FINQ has two elements, the FINST instruction queue (FIQ) and the FINST data queue (FDQ). ADVAST places instructions in FIQ, with an associated address or data element in FDQ. FINST generates a microsequence for PE control and broadcasts it to the PEs. The PEs operate in lockstep, simultaneously performing the operations specified by the microsequence.

Memory Service Unit. The memory service unit (MSU) receives all requests for storage access from the FINST, the ILA, and the I/O subsystem. It establishes priority and resolves conflicts among these units. The MSU transmits the address to memory and initiates the memory cycle.

The Array Processor

The 64 processing units comprising the ILLIAC IV array processor are identical. The processing units are composed of three parts (Figure 6.3): (a) the processing element (PE), which executes array instructions; (b) the memory logic unit (MLU), which coordinates PE and I/O requests for memory accesses; and (c) the processing element memory (PEM), which holds 2048 64-bit words.

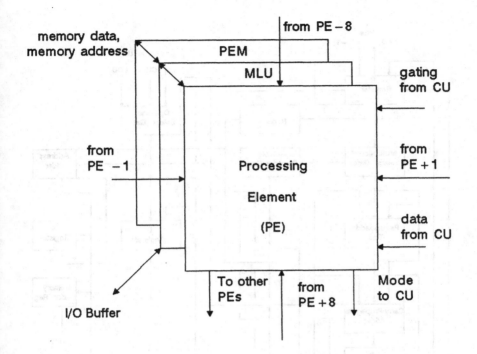

Figure 6.3 Processing unit

Processing Element. The processing element implements the operations specified by the microsequence generated in the control unit final station. With the exception of mode control and several operations sensitive to data-dependent register settings, all PEs perform identically. The PE fixed-point instructions and logical instructions operate on data 8-bits, 32-bits, or 64-bits long. Floating-point operations are performed on 32-bit and 64-bit data. The major components of the PE are: (a) registers, (b) barrel switch, (c) adder, and (d) address adder (Figure 6.4).

Registers. The processing element has five 64-bit data registers (A, B, C, R, and S)and an 8-bit mode register.

The A register supplies one operand to the adder, multiplier, and logic unit. It receives the result of the arithmetic or logical operation.

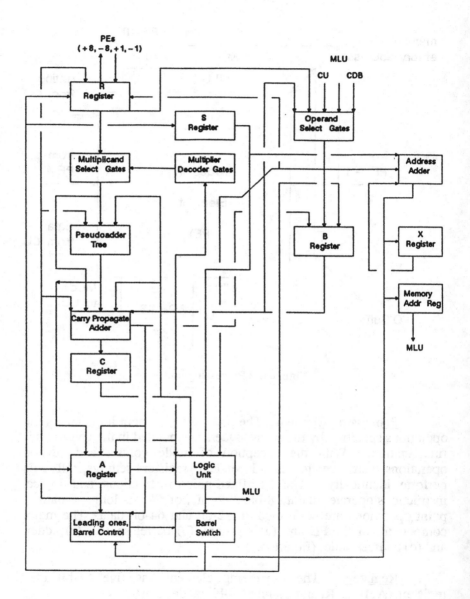

Figure 6.4 Processing element

The B register supplies the second operand to the adder and logic unit. It receives the low order part of the double precision result of a multiply instruction. In a divide instruction, the B register supplies the lower order part of a double precision dividend and receives the remainder.

The C register receives carries from the adder and supplies them to both adder and logic units.

The R register receives data routed from another PE and is used as a temporary register by the PE hardware. For example, the multiply instruction uses the R register to hold a mask.

The S register stores data under program control. It receives data from the barrel switch and supplies data to the address adder and the logic unit.

The mode register is eight bits long. Any single mode bit may be transmitted to, or received from, the CU. Two bits control gating of 32-bit or 64-bit operands to the A register, the S register, and the memory information register (MIR). If these bits are not set, the PE operations which store results in the A register, S register, or MIR are effectively null operations. Another two bits store the status of arithmetic operations (e.g. overflow). The remaining four bits hold test results.

Barrel Switch. The barrel switch is a circular right-shift register which can shift 64-bit or 32-bit quantities in one cycle. Shifts are performed either in end-around (circular) mode or in end-off mode. Shifts, performed in end-off mode, lose bits shifted beyond the end of the register and receive zeros in positions shifted into the register. A left shift of k positions is effected as a right shift of 64-k positions. The barrel switch receives input from the logic unit and places its output on an output bus available to the A register, B register, R register, and S register. The *barrel switch control* receives inputs from the *address adder*, the *carry propagate adder*, and the *leading one detector*. The barrel switch aligns data fields, performs binary point alignment prior to floating-point addition, and normalizes the results of floating-point addition.

The barrel switch is implemented in three levels of logic. Each level can shift one of four possible amounts. The first level shifts 0,

16, 32, or 48 bits. The second level shifts 0, 4, 8, or 12 bits. The third level shifts 0, 1, 2, or 3 bits. Two bits at a time of the 6-bit shift count, k, are sent to each of the three levels. This coding is equivalent to expressing the shift count as a 3 digit number in base 4.

For example, if k is 37, then in binary,

$k = 100101$,

and the 2-bit fields sent to the three levels of shift control are

$l_1 = 10$, $l_2 = 01$, $l_3 = 01$.

These values direct a first-level shift of 32, a second-level shift of 4, and a third-level shift of 1. The total number of positions shifted is 37.

Adder. The adder is designed for use by add and multiply instructions. The adder operates in carry-propagate mode for add instructions and as the final-stage adder for multiply instructions. The adder design is further optimized for the most frequently occurring instruction type: normalized unrounded. Additional clock cycles are required for additions with rounding. A 64-bit normalized floating-point addition requires 250 nanoseconds.

Multiplication is performed iteratively using the adder in carry-save mode. The 64 PEs must all complete their multiplications on the same cycle. Therefore, the multiply algorithm of the ÍLLIAC IV can not take advantage of recoding to eliminate strings of ones, as different PEs would complete at different times. Instead, a constant time algorithm is used.

The multiplier is recoded two bits at a time. An 8-bit recoded input addend is sent to the pseudoadder tree. The B register, containing the high-order bits of the multiplier and the low-order bits of the partial product, is shifted right eight bits by the barrel shifter. This iteration is repeated six times, using the carry save adder to form the sequence of partial products. A final addition, using the carry propagate adder, generates the product. The algorithm requires nine cycles:

1. Calculate the sign and the exponent; recode the eight least-significant bits of the multiplier (bits 0-7); and shift the

multiplier right by eight bits, discarding the least-significant bits (bits 0-7).

2. Input addends to the pseudoadder tree based on the previously recoded multiplier bits; recode the eight least-significant bits of the multiplier (bits 8-15); shift right by eight bits the remaining most-significant bits of the multiplier (bits 8-47), discarding the least-significant bits (bits 8-15); and place the eight least-significant bits of the partial product in positions 32-40 of the multiplier register.

3-6. Input addends to pseudoadder tree based on the previously recoded multiplier bits; recode eight least significant bits of multiplier (bits 16-23, 24-31, 32-39, 40-47); shift right by eight bits the least-significant bits of the partial product (bits 0-7, 0-15, 0-23, 0-31) and the remaining most-significant bits of the multiplier (bits 16-47, 24-47, 32-47, 40-47), discarding the least significant bits (bits 16-23, 24-31, 32-39, 40-47); and place the eight least significant bits of the partial product in the multiplier register, positions 32-40.

7. Input addends to the pseudoadder tree based on the previously recoded multiplier bits; shift right by eight bits the least-significant bits of the partial product (bits 0-39); and place the eight least-significant bits of the partial product in positions 32-40 of the multiplier register.

8. Use the carry-propagate circuitry to form the 56 most-significant bits of the product.

9. Normalize the sum.

Address adder. The address adder is used for indexing, allowing individual PEs to reference different locations during a memory cycle. It receives inputs from the X register, S register, and operand select gates. The input and output paths of the address adder are independent of the arithmetic data flow, allowing the address adder to operate concurrently with PE arithmetic functions.

Memory Logic Unit. The memory logic unit (MLU) controls all data transfers between the PE and the control unit or PE memory (Figure 6.3). I/O transfers cause some PE memory units to be busy while others are free. If the memory is busy, the MLU provides a buffer register to accept information from the PE.

Processing Element Memory. A processing element memory (PEM) is associated with each PE. The PEM holds 2048 64-bit words, with a storage cycle time of 250 nanoseconds and an access time of 200 nanoseconds. Monitor and control programs are loaded into the first 128 words of each PE. These data are write protected by setting the CU write protect bit.

INSTRUCTION SET

The ILLIAC IV has two types of instructions: (a) ADVAST instructions, which are executed in the advanced station of the control unit; and (b) FINST instructions, which are executed in the final station of the control unit. ADVAST instructions are used for housekeeping functions such as those of the operating system, address and index generation, and loop control. FINST instructions direct the PE array to perform arithmetic and logical operations of the application program.

Instruction Format

All ILLIAC IV instructions, whether ADVAST (CU program) or FINST (PE program) are 32 bits long (Figure 6.5). Both the CU and the PE are complete processors, and their instruction sets have overlapping functions. Although their functions overlap, the instructions are executed on different processors and are not redundant.

PE Instructions

The ILLIAC IV processor elements are complex machines with 169 instructions. Some of the major instructions are described below.

Routing Instructions. The PE routing instruction sends data a distance D, from PE_i to the R register of $PE_{(i+D)mod\ 64}$, for each of the 64 PEs. The data source is one of the A, B, R, S, or X registers.

5	3	8	2	1	1	4	8
op code a	Index	skip field	op'nd 1	global/ local	parity	op code b	op'nd 2

ADVAST INSTRUCTION FORMAT

5	3	4	1	3	16
op code a	Index	op code b	parity	address use	address

FINST/PE INSTRUCTION FORMAT

Figure 6.5 Instruction formats

Arithmetic Instructions. The arithmetic instructions for PE execution operate in several different modes and on several data types, depending on instruction modifier bits and on machine state. A global machine state, indicated by the ADVAST control register, is communicated to each PE with each instruction. The choice of 32-bit or 64-bit floating-point arithmetic is controlled by the *32-bit-mode* bit of the ACR and is set by an ADVAST instruction. When operating in 32-bit mode, unless otherwise specified, two 32-bit operations are performed on each 64-bit word. The *enable bits* of a PE's mode register control whether the result of an arithmetic operation will change the setting of the A register. The PE mode register is set locally by test instructions in each PE. Within the PE instruction code, modifiers indicate whether or not:

1. An instruction is fixed point or floating point, M;

2. An instruction operates with unsigned or signed numbers, A;

3. An instruction's result is rounded, R; and

4. An instruction's result is normalized (after it has been rounded, if specified), N.

Instructions are available for addition, subtraction, multiplication, and division. Each of these instructions may be used with modifiers in one of the combinations listed below:

1. (None) : Floating point, signed, unnormalized, unrounded;

2. MA: Fixed point, unsigned, unrounded;

3. NA: Floating point, unsigned, normalized, unrounded;

4. RA: Floating point, signed, unnormalized, rounded;

5. RM: Fixed point, signed, rounded;

6. RMA: Fixed point, unsigned, rounded;

7. RN: Floating point, signed, normalized, rounded; and

8. RNA: Floating point, unsigned, normalized, rounded.

Two other variants of arithmetic data format are available for addition and subtraction operations. A *byte format* instruction performs the indicated operation on corresponding 8-bit bytes of 64-bit operands. A *full word* format instruction performs the indicated operation on 64-bit unsigned integer quantities, regardless of the setting of the 32-bit-mode bit.

Test Instructions. Thirty two test instructions are provided in the PE. They are formed by combining the following modifiers:

T=I or J: In 64-bit mode, the test result is stored in I or J. In 32-bit mode, the second test result is stored in G or H.

U=G or L: Perform arithmetic test for greater or less.

V=E, G, or L: Perform logical test for equal, greater, or less.

A=A: Perform arithmetic test of the A register.

W=S or X: Test the S or X register.

X=L or M: Perform logical test of the full-word or only the mantissa part of the A register.

Y=O or Z: Test A register for all ones or all zeros.

There are four different families of test instructions. A prototype instruction for each family is shown below. An instruction is defined by the properties of the options chosen in filling out the prototype.

1. T A U: Arithmetic test of A register for greater or less; result sent to I or J bit in the PE mode register;

2. T X V: Logical test of A register (full or mantissa only) for equal, greater, or less; result sent to I or J bit in the PE mode register;

3. T X Y: Logical test of A register (full or mantissa only) for all ones or all zeros; result sent to I or J bit in the PE mode register; and

4. T W V: Arithmetic test of the S or X register for equal, greater, or less; result sent to I or J bit in the PE mode register.

Shift Instructions. Eight variations of shift instructions are available as combinations of the following modifiers:

A or AB: Shift involves the A register or the A register and the B register.

F or M: The full register participates or only the mantissa participates.

L or R: The shift is to the left or to the right.

Additionally, the A register may be end-around shifted (rotated) left or right.

Boolean Instructions. The ILLIAC IV PE Boolean operations replace the A register with the specified function of the A register and the storage address, X. The functions available are:

(a) and, (b) and not, (c) exclusive or, (d) equivalence, (e) not and, (f) not and not, (g) not or, (h) not or not, (i) or, and (j) or not.

CHAPTER 7

THE CRAY-1

PERSPECTIVE

The CDC 6600, CDC 7600, and IBM 360/91 performed at peak speed when processing highly regular data. Programmers, intent on maximizing performance, optimized inner loops by counting machine cycles to assure that memory and register conflicts were minimized and that pipelines were full. Both manual and compiler techniques were aimed at creating machine code enabling loops to take advantage of the IBM 360/91 hardware's loop mode. Similar approaches were employed with the CDC 7600. STACKLIB, a collection of subroutines which processed arrays of data, was developed to permit the CDC 7600 to operate at maximum speed. Utilizing tightly coded loops to process vectors of data suggested the development of a hardware implementation.

The Cray-1, initially delivered in 1976, is the first of a family of general purpose vector processor machines from Cray Research Inc. The Cray-1 and its successors, the Cray-XMP and the Cray-2, are optimized to solve large-scale problems in science and engineering. In addition to high speed circuitry, long word length, and large memory, the systems feature a vector processing architecture and 12 pipelined functional units.

ARCHITECTURE

Figure 7.1 illustrates the organization of the Cray-1 processor. Word size is 64 bits. The original machine had a memory capacity of 1 megaword. Newer models may have up to 16 megawords. The clock cycle of the Cray-1 is 12.5 nanoseconds. Major elements of the Cray-1 include:

1. Twelve pipelined function units;

2. Eight address (A) registers;

3. 64 intermediate (B) registers;

4. Eight scalar (S) registers;

5. 64 scalar intermediate (T) registers;

6. Eight vector (V) floating point registers, each with 64 elements per register;

7. Four instruction buffers; and

8. 1,048,576 words of single error correction--double error detection memory.

An instruction control mechanism is responsible for instruction issue and for overlapping vector processing with scalar and address processing. The registers are specialized by function, avoiding conflicts among vector, scalar, and addressing instructions.

Just as the CDC 6600 and CDC 7600 are register oriented machines, so is the Cray-1. Operands of arithmetic and logical operations must be resident in registers. Transfer of data between the registers and storage is a separate task from numerical computation. Programming techniques and compiler mechanisms, used on the CDC 6600 and CDC 7600 for allocating and managing registers, are equally useful on the Cray-1.

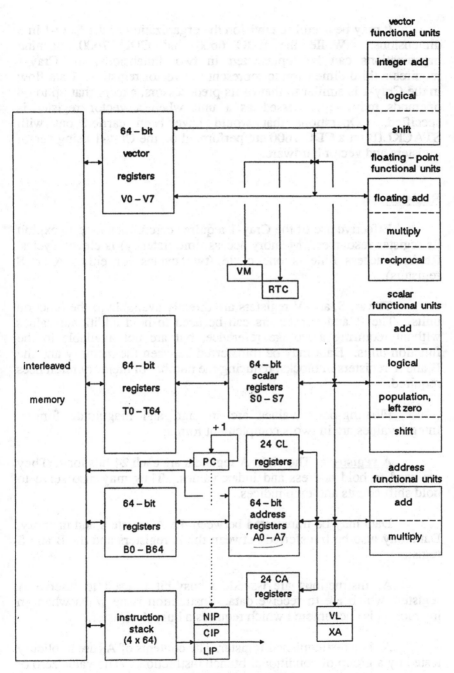

Figure 7.1 The Cray processor

It may be useful to envision the organization of the Cray-1 in 3 dimensions. While the CDC 6600 and CDC 7600 machine organizations can be represented in two dimensions, the Cray-1 requires a third dimension to represent the vector registers. Data flow in the Cray-1 is similar to that of its predecessors, except that up to 64 operands may be processed as a unit when a vector register is specified. Operations that would have been carried out with STACKLIB on a CDC 7600 are performed on the Cray-1 using vector registers and vector hardware.

Registers

Effective use of the Cray-1 requires careful planning to exploit its register resources. Memory access time (latency) is eleven cycles. Register access time is one cycle (two cycles for either A or S registers).

The A, S, and V registers are directly available to the function units. The B and T registers can be used to hold additional values without requiring a storage reference, but are not available to the function units. Data may be transferred between the memory and the B and T registers in blocks, reducing the number of memory references required.

Floating-point values are in sign and magnitude format. Integer values are in two's complement format.

A registers. The eight A registers are each 24 bits long. They are used to hold address and index values. They may also serve to hold shift counts and loop indices.

Data may be transferred between the A registers and memory. Data may also be transferred between the A registers and the B and S registers.

As instructions are issued, a busy-bit is used to reserve A registers which are to receive data. Instruction issue waits when an instruction is encountered which requires a busy A register.

A_0 is a distinguished register. The contents of A_0 are implicitly tested by a group of conditional branch instructions. The value zero or

2^{63} (respectively) is automatically supplied when A_0 is specified in the j or k field of an instruction.

B registers. The 64 B registers are each 24 bits long and serve as temporary storage for the A registers. Transfers between the A and B registers require only 1 cycle. Transfers between the B registers and memory occur in blocks, during which time no instructions are issued.

Register B_0 is used to receive the return address (i.e. the address of the next instruction) when a return jump instruction is executed.

S registers. The eight S registers are each 64 bits long and are the processor's scalar registers. They supply operands to, and receive results from, scalar floating-point, integer, and logical operations. They also supply the scalar operand in mixed scalar/vector operations.

Data may be transferred between the S registers and the A, T, and V registers. The S registers also can receive the contents of the vector-mask register (VM) and the clock register.

Only one S register can receive a result during a cycle. Instruction issue is delayed one cycle if it would have resulted in a data conflict (two arriving data elements) at the S registers.

S_0 is a distinguished register. The contents of S_0 are implicitly tested by a group of conditional branch instructions. S_0 is the result register for one set of shift instructions. When S_0 is specified in the j or k field of an instruction, the value zero or 2^{63} (respectively) is automatically supplied.

T registers. The 64 T registers are each 64 bits long and serve as temporary storage for the S registers. Transfers between the A and B registers require only one cycle. Transfers between the T registers and memory occur in blocks, during which time no instructions are issued.

V registers. The eight V registers are each comprised of 64 elements, each 64 bits long. They are used, with the pipelined function units, for vector operations. Under control of the vector-length register, from 1 to 64 elements may participate in a vector operation. The Cray-1 derives most of its speed advantage from its ability to exploit pipelining by amortizing the arithmetic startup time over a sequence of operations.

Several pipelines may proceed concurrently. In a single cycle, a vector register can both sink and source an operand. One function unit may use the output of another function unit as its input. This results in *chaining*, a term used to describe the routing of a (processed) data stream through a series of function units.

When a vector operation begins, the result register is marked busy and may not participate in another operation until marked free. An exception is made during the "chain slot" time. At chain slot time, a vector register, despite being marked busy, may serve as an operand source for another vector operation.

VL register. The vector-length register (VL) specifies the number of elements of a vector which are to be processed; $0 \leq VL \leq 64$.

VM register. The vector-mask register (VM), 64 bits long, allows conditional operations to be effected within a vector. This is analogous to the masked operations available on the ILLIAC IV or on the MPP. The status of the mask at the start of the vector operation controls execution. Each bit position of the mask controls the corresponding element of a vector register. Where a 1-bit is present, the operation is performed; where a 0-bit is present, the operation is skipped. VM may be set from an S register or may reflect the results of a test of vector register elements.

Instruction Format

The Cray-1 instruction format is quite similar to that of the CDC 6600. Instructions are either 16 or 32 bits long. All instructions contain a seven bit operation code. In the short format (16 bit) instructions, the remaining nine bits either specify the two operand registers and the result register, or specify a result register and a short (six-bit) constant value. Long format instructions are necessary when a memory address or a long constant must be specified within the instruction. Figure 7.2 illustrates the instruction formats.

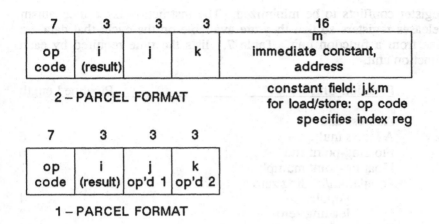

Figure 7.2 Instruction Formats

Vector Instruction Types

There are three types of vector instructions:

1. Instructions used to load or store the vector registers; specifying transfers between the vector registers and memory;

2. Instructions specifying vector operations with vector register inputs; with the operation carried out on corresponding elements of the vector registers; and

3. Instructions specifying vector operations with vector and scalar inputs; with the operation carried out on the scalar and successive elements of the vector register.

Multiple Function Units

The Cray-1 contains twelve pipelined function units. The function units are independent and may operate concurrently. Each function unit can accept a new set of operands every cycle and produces a result a fixed number of cycles later. The known time required by each function unit allows register scheduling delays and register conflicts to be minimized. The instruction issue mechanism releases registers so that they are available on the cycle that data are due from a function unit. Table 7.1 lists the time required by each function unit.

Function Unit	Pipeline Length
Address add	2
Address multiply	6
Floating-point add	6
Floating-point multiply	7
Population/leading zero	
population	4
leading zero	3
Reciprocal approximation	14
Scalar add	3
Scalar logical	1
Scalar shift	
single	2
double	3
Vector add	3
Vector logical	2
Vector shift	4

Table 7.1 Function Unit Timing

Address add unit. The address add unit computes the sum or difference of two 24-bit quantities in the A registers.

Address multiply unit. The address multiply unit computes the (24-bit) product of two 24-bit quantities in the A registers.

Floating-point add unit. The floating-point add unit computes the sum of two 64-bit floating-point quantities. In scalar mode, both operands are in the S registers, and the result is returned to an S register. In vector mode, either both operands are in the V registers (vector plus vector) or one operand is in a V register and the second operand is in an S register (vector plus scalar). The result is returned to a V register.

Floating-point multiply unit. The floating-point multiply unit computes the full-precision or half-precision product of two floating-point operands. The full-precision product may optionally be rounded in the low-order bit position. The floating-point multiply unit also computes 2 - $operand_1$ * $operand_2$ for the reciprocal iteration used to perform division. As in the floating-point add unit, in scalar mode both operands are in the S registers, with the result returned to an S register. In vector mode, either both operands are in the V registers (vector times vector) or one operand is in a V register and the second operand is in an S register (vector times scalar). The result is returned to a V register.

The floating-point multiply unit creates the 48-bit x 48-bit binary product matrix from the input operands. Each row is the partial product of the multiplicand with the corresponding multiplier bit. These partial products, in the form of a parallelogram, are then added together to form the complete 96-bit product. Only the rightmost 48 bits will be used in the 64-bit floating point representation. Accordingly, the low order portion of the pyramid is truncated, as shown in Figure 7.3. A constant, equal to the average value of the sum of the truncated quantities, is added to the product sum to remove the negative bias caused by truncation.

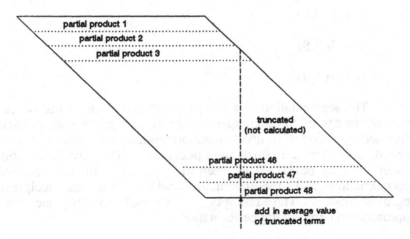

Figure 7.3 Multiply pyramid

Population/leading-zero unit. The population count is the number of one-bits present in a 64-bit operand. The leading-zero count is the number of zero-bits present before the leftmost 1-bit of a 64-bit operand. The operand is in an S register, and the (seven-bit) result is returned to an A register.

Reciprocal approximation unit. The reciprocal approximation unit computes the approximate reciprocal of its one operand, correct to 30 bits, . For a scalar operation, the S registers contain both the operand and the result. For a vector operation, the V registers contain the operand and result.

Division is performed by multiplying the reciprocal approximation by the dividend, yielding a half-precision quotient. Calculation of a full-precision quotient requires a correction factor which is produced by the divide iteration instruction (a variant of the multiply instruction which performs one step of a Newton iteration). The correction factor is used to multiply the half-precision quotient to yield a full-precision quotient. The sequence of instructions necessary to divide the contents of register S_5 by the contents of register S_2 is:

$$S_1 = 1 / S_2$$

$$S_3 = 2 - S_1 * S_2$$

$$S_4 = S_5 * S_1$$

$$S_6 = S_3 * S_4$$

The segmentation of a full-precision divide into 4 instructions takes advantage of the high speed multiply unit and allows efficient pipelined operation. The divide iteration produces the correction factor needed only for the final multiplication. The divide iteration instruction may be placed between the calculation of the reciprocal approximation and the instruction which uses the reciprocal approximation. The multiply is chained to the reciprocal approximation, improving performance.

Scalar add unit. The scalar add unit computes the 64-bit sum or difference of two integer quantities in the S registers.

Scalar logical unit.. The scalar logical unit performs a specified boolean operation on the corresponding bits of its two 64-bit operands. The scalar logical unit may also be used to generate a mask field. Operands and results are in the S registers. S_j and S_k contain the operand values (for the merge instruction S_i also contains an operand value), and S_i receives the result.

If $j = 0$ (i.e. S_0 is specified for S_j), then the value 0 (64 binary zeros) is supplied as the first operand in lieu of S_0. If $k = 0$ (i.e. S_0 is specified for S_k), then 2^{63} (a one followed by 63 zeros) is supplied as the second operand in lieu of S_0.

The boolean operations available include: (a) and; (b) and not; (c) exclusive or; (d) or; (e) equivalence; and (f) merge, $S_{i,n} = (S_{k,n} .and. S_{j,n}) .or. (\sim S_{k,n} .and. S_i)$.

Scalar shift unit. The scalar shift function unit shifts the contents of a register left or right with zero fill; circular shifts a register or shifts two concatenated registers left or right with zero fill.

Vector add unit. The vector add unit computes the 64-bit vector sum or difference of two operands. The operands may both be vector elements (in the V registers), or the first operand may be a scalar (in an S register). The vector-length register indicates the number of elements participating in the operation.

Vector logical unit. The vector logical unit performs a specified boolean operation on the corresponding bits of its two 64-bit operands. As is the case with the vector add, the first operand may be a scalar (in an S register). The vector-length register indicates the number of elements participating in the operation.

The operations available in the vector logical unit are: (a) and, (b) exclusive or, (c) or, (d) merge, and (e) generate vector mask.

The merge operation replaces V_i by either the first operand (S_j or the elements of V_j) or the second operand (V_k), depending on whether the corresponding vector-mask register bit is a one or a zero, respectively.

$$V_{i,n} = (VM_n \text{ .and. } V_{j,n}) \text{ .or. } (\sim VM_n \text{ .and. } V_{k,n})$$

$$V_{i,n} = (VM_n \text{ .and. } S_j) \text{.or.} (\sim VM_n \text{ .and. } V_{k,n})$$

The generate vector mask operation performs a test on the elements of the operand vector register and sets the corresponding bit of VM to indicate whether the test succeeded or failed. The tests possible are: (a) equal zero, (b) not equal zero, (c) greater than zero, and (d) less than zero.

Vector shift unit. The vector shift unit performs shifts on the elements of the specified operand register either individually, or as if all vector element registers were a single unit.

IMPLEMENTATION PHILOSOPHY

Instruction Processing

The Cray-1 instruction processing mechanism is designed to issue instructions every cycle, except when there are resource conflicts. The components of the instruction processing mechanism are: (a) current instruction register, (b) lower instruction register, (c) next instruction register, (d) program counter, and (e) four instruction buffers (Figure 7.4).

Current Instruction Register. The current instruction register (CIR) is 16 bits long. When an instruction reaches the CIR, it is certain to be issued after any necessary delays. Execution control lines are distributed from the CIR. The CIR receives instructions from the next instruction register.

Lower Instruction Register. The lower instruction register (LIR) is 16 bits long and contains the low order half of long format (32 bit) instructions. By placing the low order half of long format instructions in the LIR, the next instruction register remains free to receive the following instruction.

Next Instruction Register. The next instruction register (NIR) is 16 bits long and is used to stage instructions between storage and the CIR.

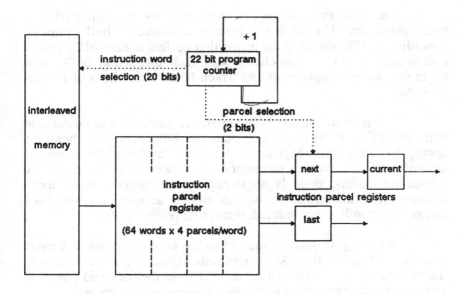

Figure 7.4 Instruction processing mechanism

Program Counter. The program counter (PC) is a 22-bit register with an associated increment unit. The PC contains the address of the instruction which is being fetched to the NIR. When the instruction arrives, the PC is incremented. Execution of a branch or exchange package replaces the PC with the address of the new instruction stream.

Instruction Buffers. The 4 instruction buffers of the Cray-1 are similar to the instruction buffer array found in the IBM 360/91. Virtual memory and instruction caches were receiving significant attention at the time the Cray-1 was designed. Their influence is apparent in the techniques employed with the instruction buffers.

Modification of the instruction stream is not effective if the modified instruction was previously loaded into an instruction buffer. A similar situation existed on the CDC 6600. The IBM 360/91, in order to maintain compatibility with lower-performance systems which did not pre-fetch instructions, contained additional circuitry to detect a change to the instruction stream and to update the instruction buffer array.

Each instruction buffer can contain 128 bytes, or up to 64 two-byte instructions. The starting address of an instruction buffer must be a multiple of 128, allowing the instruction buffers to map 512 bytes of contiguous memory. Associated with each instruction buffer is a beginning address register (BAR) which holds the address of its first location.

When an instruction is required, the four BARs are compared with the PC. If there is a match, the NIR is loaded from the appropriate instruction buffer. Forward and backward branches are accommodated. When instruction sequences are found in the instruction buffers, there is no storage access delay. When loops execute within the instruction buffers, storage accesses are eliminated and storage conflicts are reduced, increasing performance.

A two cycle delay ensues when the next instruction is located in a different buffer than the current instruction. If there is no match, the next instruction must first be fetched from memory and placed in an instruction buffer before instruction processing can proceed.

Instruction buffers are used in rotation. The least recently filled instruction buffer is selected for use when the next instruction is not already in a buffer. An instruction buffer is refilled with 4 words (32 bytes) per clock cycle. The instruction buffer is refilled circularly, beginning with the 4-word group containing the next instruction (as indicated by the PC). As soon as the next instruction is loaded into the instruction buffer, instruction processing resumes. The instruction buffer continues to be loaded with consecutive groups of 4 words until its end is reached. As indicated by the BAR, fetching continues at the beginning of the instruction buffer until the buffer is full.

Register and function unit reservation

The Cray-1 is quite similar to the CDC 6600 in its handling of register and function unit reservations. As vector instructions are issued, the registers and function units used by them are marked reserved. The function unit will be kept busy for the length of the vector. The operand register will be kept busy transmitting successive vector elements at a one per cycle rate.

When a vector instruction is ready for issue, the required function unit and registers are checked for availability. If the required registers or function unit are marked reserved, the instruction is delayed until the reservations are released. Instructions which are independent of near-term previous instructions, that is, have no registers in common and use different function units, face no instruction issue delays.

An example of an operand register conflict is:

$$V_1 = V_2 * V_3$$

$$V_4 = V_5 + V_2$$

The second instruction specifies V_2 as an operand register. V_2 is reserved by the first instruction and not available until the conclusion of the first instruction. The time at which V_2 will be released is predictable since function unit times are fixed (the floating-point multiply time is seven cycles) and registers operate at a one access per cycle rate. This allows instruction issue to proceed immediately when a reservation is released. If the reservation release was not predictable, then instruction issue could not proceed until notification of the register release had been received, requiring an additional delay of one cycle.

An example of a function unit conflict is:

$$V_1 = V_2 * V_3$$

$$V_4 = V_5 * V_6$$

The second instruction specifies a floating-point multiply. The floating-point multiply unit is marked reserved by the first instruction and will not be free until all vector elements are multiplied. As was the case with the operand register conflict in the previous example, the time when the reservation will be released is predictable. Instruction issue will occur on the cycle that the function unit becomes available.

The instructions below are independent and do not cause any register or function unit reservation conflicts:

$$V_1 = V_2 * V_3$$

$$V_4 = V_5 + V_6$$

Vector Processing

Peak performance of the Cray-1 is only attained in the vector processing mode. When operating in this mode, instruction startup overhead is amortized over a vector sequence as long as 64 operations. After an initial delay due to pipeline length, termed latency, results are produced at a rate of one per cycle. The capability of *chaining* operations (connecting the output of one function unit to the input of another function unit) can result in some calculations being performed at a rate of 2 operations per clock cycle, or 160 megaflops (million floating-point operations per second). Chaining is similar to data forwarding performed by the common data bus of the IBM 360 model 91.

Vector result registers are reserved at the beginning of an operation and not released until the final result is received. Chaining is possible when an instruction requires vector results and is ready for issue at the time that the first vector result arrives (*chain slot time*). The instruction processing unit detects the use of an operand register which is reserved as a result register. If the registers match and the instruction is ready at chain slot time, it is issued and the specified function unit receives operands at the same time as they are received by the vector register (Figure 7.5).

The following example illustrates the effect of chaining [CRA78]:

$VL = 64$ Set vector length to 64

$V_0 = A$ Fetch 64 values of A

$V_1 = V_0 < A_7$ Left shift

$V_3 = V_1 \& V_2$ Logical product

$V_5 = V_3 + V_4$ Integer sum

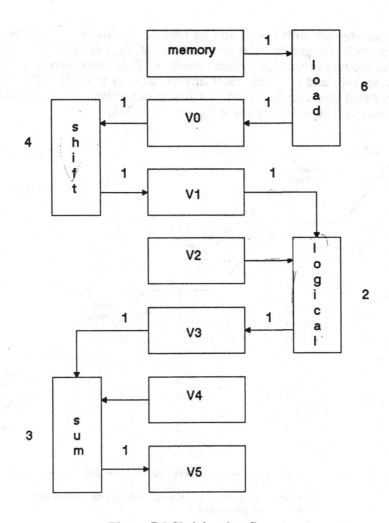

Figure 7.5 Chaining data flow

As indicated in Figure 7.6, if chaining was not available, instruction issue would be delayed for each vector instruction after the vector load. The function unit times for left shift, logical product, and integer sum are, four cycles, two cycles, and three cycles, respectively. An additional cycle is required to move elements in each direction between a vector register and a function unit. The first operand, A_1, arrives at $V_{0,0}$ at cycle 8, and A_{64} arrives at $V_{0,63}$ at cycle 71. Only then can the left shift instruction be issued. Its first result arrives at $V_{1,0}$ at cycle 78, and its final result arrives at $V_{1,63}$ at cycle 141. The logical product instruction is then issued. Its first result arrives at $V_{3,0}$ at cycle 146, and its final result arrives at $V_{3,63}$ at cycle 209. The integer sum can then be issued. Its first result arrives at $V_{5,0}$ at cycle 215, and its final result arrives at $V_{5,63}$ at cycle 278.

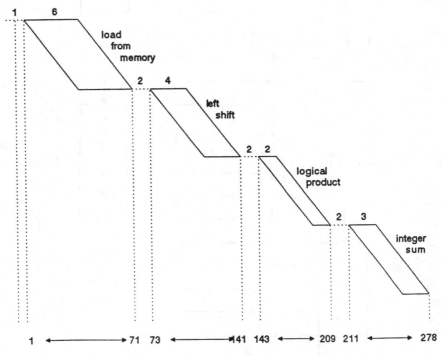

Times given are for the start and completion of data movement within each vector instruction.

Figure 7.6 Non-chain timing

The timing is dramatically different with chaining (Figure 7.7). The vector load again results in the first operand arriving at $V_{0,0}$ at cycle 8. The shift instruction is issued in time for the function unit to receive its first operand at cycle 9. The first result element of the shift arrives at $V_{1,0}$ at cycle 14. The logical product is similarly issued sufficiently early so that its first operand arrives at the function unit at cycle 15. Its first result element is returned to $V_{3,0}$ at cycle 18. The add instruction is also issued in time for the function unit to receive its first operand at cycle 19. The first result element of the integer sum unit arrives at $V_{5,0}$ at cycle 23. The final (64th) result element arrives at $V_{5,63}$ at cycle 86.

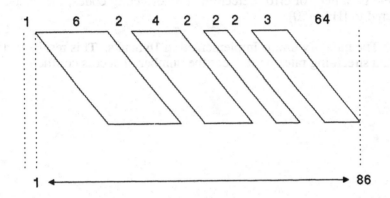

Figure 7.7 Chaining

Not counting the vector load instruction, three operations are performed on each of 64 vector elements. Without chaining, a total of 192 operations are performed in 278 cycles, at an average rate of .69 operation per cycle. Chaining allows 192 operations to be performed in 86 cycles, an average rate of 2.2 operations per cycle.

Memory

The memory system of the Cray-1 represents a breakthrough in the size and performance of a directly addressable main memory. The first Cray-1 models (The Cray-1A) address up to 1,048,576 eight-byte words with a 50 nanosecond memory cycle time (4 central processor cycles). Access time to the central processor is eleven cycles. The early models use bipolar memory technology which store 1024 bits on a chip. Later models allow increased addressable memory, up to 16,777,216 words, and use high speed CMOS chips which each store 262,144 bits.

Single error correction--double error detection is implemented in the memory by an 8-bit code associated with each 64-bit data word. The code is generated when a word is stored. When a data word is fetched, the code is used to determine whether any errors have occurred. Single-bit errors may be corrected without loss of data. All double-bit errors are detected and can initiate an interrupt. For a complete treatment of error detection and correcting codes, the reader is referred to [HAM50].

The memory unit is implemented in 16 banks. This results in a high data streaming rate and reduces the number of access conflicts.

CHAPTER 8

THE CYBER 205

PERSPECTIVE

The Control Data Corporation CYBER 205 is a direct descendant of the STAR-100. Many improvements, most notably the inclusion of a scalar processor, evolved from experience with the STAR-100. Scalar computations on the STAR-100 were inefficient due to the long latency of the vector pipelines. A series of scalar floating-point additions was ten times slower than the same number of additions performed in vector mode. On the CYBER-205, register operations involving scalars need not use the pipelines. These computations are performed by the set of independent function units within the scalar processor.

Advances in technology resulted in improved reliability as well as increased capacity and increased capability. This chapter highlights the architectural improvements embodied in the

CYBER 205 and differences between the CYBER-205 and the STAR-100.

ARCHITECTURE

The architecture of the CYBER 205 (Figure 8.1) is similar to that of the STAR-100. Significant architectural improvements include the addition of a scalar processor and related hardware, as well as the availability of up to four floating-point pipelines. The major changes are:

1. A scalar processor executes instruction sequences which are not appropriate for vector mode. The scalar processor contains independent function units.

2. An instruction issue unit coordinates instruction processing between the scalar processor and the vector processor. It decodes instructions for both the scalar processor and the vector processor, and it can issue a scalar instruction every minor cycle unless there is a conflict.

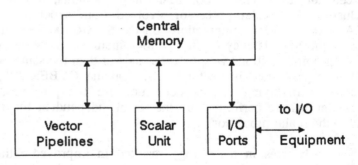

Figure 8.1 The CYBER 205

3. A load/store unit controls the transfer of data between the register file and storage. It also acts as a buffer, holding data when storage cycle conflicts occur. The load/store unit is similar to the floating-point buffers and store data buffers of the IBM 360/91.

4. The CYBER 205 has 1, 2, or 4 identical floating-point pipelines.

5. The memory access width is doubled from a superword (512 bits) to two superwords (1024 bits) to provide the data rate needed when four pipelines operate concurrently.

The Scalar Processor

The scalar processor of the CYBER 205 is analogous to the instruction processor of the IBM 360 model 91. The scalar processor is responsible for decoding all instructions. Vector and string instructions are issued to the vector processor for execution. Other instructions are executed within the scalar processor. Microcode is used to control three scalar processor functions: (a) associative register operations, (b) floating-point arithmetic, and (c) scalar instruction processing. The major elements of the scalar processor (Figure 8.2) are:

1. A register file;

2. A priority unit;

3. A load/store unit;

4. An instruction processing unit; and

5. A floating-point unit.

Register File. The Cyber 205 register file has 256 entries of 64-bit words. Two read operations and one write operation can be performed in the register file each minor cycle. Either the vector processor or the scalar processor, but not both at one time, can access the register file.

The *shortstop* path allows a scalar result to be used as an operand for a subsequent instruction at the same time as it is being stored in the register file. The instruction processing unit detects opportunities for using the shortstop path and establishes the data routing. Use of the shortstop path saves up to 3 cycles, as data do not have to return from the register file.

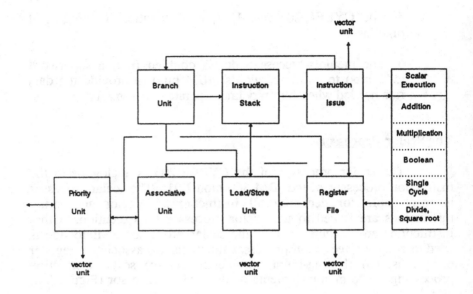

Figure 8.2 Scalar processor

Priority Unit. The priority unit handles all memory transfers of the scalar processor. The priority unit issues a request to memory providing: (a) there is no higher priority request, (b) the virtual address matches an associative register entry, and (c) the required memory banks are not busy. When the priority unit issues a request to memory, it responds to the originating unit with an *accept*.

When a busy indication is received in response to a request, the priority unit waits four cycles and then retries memory. If memory access requests involved only a single bank, a delay of four cycles (equal to the memory cycle time) would be excessive. However, the width of a memory bank is a half word (32 data bits), and so a two superword memory access (1024 data bits) involves 32 memory banks. With wide requests, involving many memory banks, it is likely that at least one of the requested banks would have begun an access cycle at the time of the request and would not be free until four cycles have passed.

Load/Store unit. The load/store unit contains six address registers. It buffers sequences of load and store operations. It processes loads at a rate of one per minor cycle and processes stores at the rate of one per two minor cycles (but requires 7 cycles for 3 consecutive stores). The load/store unit requires additional time for instructions which modify words or parts of words.

Instruction Processing Unit. The CYBER 205 instruction stack is eight swords long, twice the capacity of the stack on the STAR-100. When an instruction is processed, the two swords after the current one are prefetched. The eight sword stack can hold six non-contiguous swords, as well as two swords of prefetched instructions. Sword addresses are kept with each stack entry. Out of stack branches do not clear the stack. Instead, the out of stack instruction is fetched and placed in the stack. If the loop is small (fits into 6 swords), it is held in the stack even though its instructions are not consecutive. Subsequent iterations of the loop occur without causing an out of stack condition.

Concurrent Vector and Scalar Operation. All instructions are decoded and issued by the instruction issue unit of the scalar processor. Vector (scalar) instructions must be checked to ensure that they do not depend on a register value which is not yet available from an instruction execution in the scalar (vector) processor. To avoid memory conflicts, load and store instructions cannot be issued when a vector instruction is executing. The instruction issue unit allows vector and scalar processors to operate concurrently when their instruction streams are independent.

If the vector processor is free when a vector instruction is decoded, and if there are no register file conflicts, the instruction is issued to the vector processor for execution. The instruction is not issued if the vector processor is busy, or if there is a register file conflict. For example, the vector instruction requires a register which has not yet received the result of a prior scalar operation).

If the vector processor is busy when a scalar instruction is decoded, and there are no register file conflicts, the instruction is issued and executed within the scalar processor. If there is a register file conflict (e.g. the scalar instruction requires a register which has not yet received the result of the current vector operation), the instruction is not issued.

Instruction Issue. This unit is more complex in the CYBER 205 than in the STAR-100 as it coordinates interactions between the scalar processor and the vector processor. If there are no conflicts, an instruction is issued every minor cycle. The instruction issue unit checks for the following conflicts:

1. Register file write conflict. The register file can accept two read operations and one write operation each cycle. An instruction is not issued if its completion time requires a write into the register file on the same cycle as another instruction currently in progress.

2. Output Operand Conflict. An instruction does not issue if its result destination is the same register file location as an ongoing instruction.

3. Source Operand Conflict. An instruction does not issue if it requires an input operand which is not yet available in the register file.

The status of the result registers of prior operations must be checked to determine whether an instruction issue conflict exists. *The result-address registers* contain the register file addresses for the results of previous instructions. If a conflict is found, the instruction is not issued until the conflict is cleared. The STAR-100's three result-address registers were the cause of a bottleneck: an instruction was not issued if a result-address register was not available. Increasing the number of result-address registers in the CYBER 205 removed the bottleneck.

Floating-Point Unit. Except for divide and square root, the scalar floating-point operations are performed in fully pipelined units. The pipelined units can accept a new pair of operands each cycle. Add, subtract, and multiply each require five pipeline cycles; logical operations require three pipeline cycles. Divide and square root are performed iteratively, and the function unit can accept new operands only after the previous computation is completed.

The Vector Processor

The vector processor of the CYBER 205 has from one to four pipelines for processing sequences of vector operands. With four pipelines, the CYBER 205 produces four 64-bit results per minor cycle, or 200,000,000 results per second. The major elements of the vector processor (Figure 8.3) are:

1. Floating-point pipelines;

2. A stream addressing pipeline;

3. A string unit;

4. A vector setup unit; and

5. A vector stream input and output.

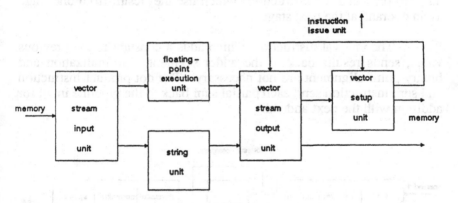

Figure 8.3 Vector processor

Floating-Point Pipelines. The CYBER 205 has from one to four floating-point pipelines. To allow flexibility in configuring and upgrading systems, all pipelines are identical (Figure 8.4). A pair of 128-bit buses provides input operands to a one-pipeline configuration. Two pairs of 64-bit operands are available with each data access. A two-pipeline configuration sends odd-numbered operands to one pipeline and even-numbered operands to the other pipeline. A pair of 256-bit buses provides input operands to a four-pipeline configuration.

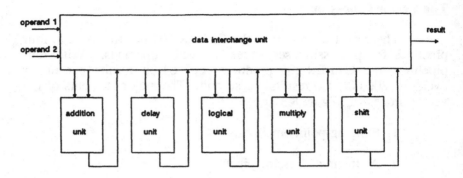

Figure 8.4 Floating-point pipeline

<u>Floating-Point Add Unit.</u> The add unit is fully segmented and accepts new operands every cycle. Two internal data paths (Figure 8.5) are provided for instructions which use the result from one stage as an operand at the next stage.

The interval instruction, which adds a constant to the previous value, sends results back to the adder segment. Normalization and binary point alignment are not necessary. The dot product instruction and sum instruction send each partial sum back to the pipeline input for addition with the next addend.

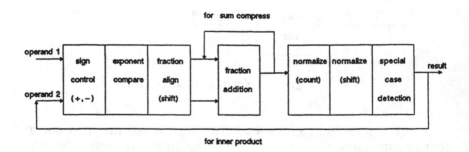

Figure 8.5 Floating-point add unit

<u>Floating-Point Multiply/Divide Unit.</u> As shown in Figure 8.6, multiply and divide circuits share the merge/complement segment.

Multiply is fully segmented and can accept new input operands every cycle. Division is iterative and only can accept input operands at the conclusion of an iteration.

The product instruction sends each partial product back to the input where it is multiplied by the next operand.

The Stream Addressing Pipeline. The function of the stream addressing pipeline within the vector processor is analogous to the function of the load/store unit within the scalar processor. Complex address patterns and a highly banked memory require a degree of oversight to ensure that data are transferred efficiently. The stream unit prefetches input data and buffers it in the vector stream input unit. It stores output data held, in a similar buffer, in the vector stream output unit.

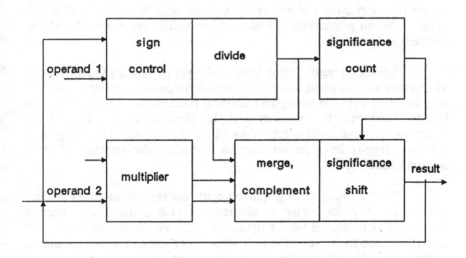

Figure 8.6 Floating-point multiply/divide unit

String Unit. The string unit receives input data from the vector stream input unit, aligns string elements, combines string elements as directed by the current string instruction, and sends the results to the vector stream output unit.

Vector Setup Unit. The vector setup unit decodes instructions, provides control fields to vector units, provides address and length parameters to the vector units, and monitors execution. These functions are performed under microprogram control.

The vector setup unit does not release the scalar processor if a vector processor instruction uses the register file during execution. Each cycle, the register file can support two reads and a write. If the register file is used by a register instruction, it can not support a simultaneous scalar instruction. If a vector processor instruction does not require the register file, other than to return a result value, an entry is made in the result address register, and the scalar processor is released. The scalar processor does not issue an instruction while it has a register conflict.

When an interrupt is processed, the vector setup unit halts the vector function units and stores the current addresses and field length values. When processing resumes, these values are restored and the instruction is restarted.

Vector Stream Input Unit and Vector Stream Output Unit. The vector stream input and vector stream output units have symmetric relationships with the string and floating-point units. They provide an interface between the memory and the pipeline units. The vector stream units supply and delete zeros in sparse vectors. They align and combine results into quarter swords, reducing the number of store accesses required.

For example, during sparse vector operations, memory fetches are made only for nonzero elements. Using the order vectors associated with sparse vector operations, the vector stream input unit provides zeros to the function unit where necessary. The vector stream output unit discards results under control of the result order vector. Only nonzero elements are stored, reducing the volume of data traffic between memory and the vector processor.

CHAPTER 9

THE MASSIVELY PARALLEL PROCESSOR

PERSPECTIVE

The Massively Parallel Processor (MPP) is a 128x128 parallel processing array computer. It was built by Goodyear Aerospace Corporation under contract to Goddard Space Flight Center and delivered in May, 1983. The MPP is a direct descendant of the ILLIAC IV and shares many of that system's advantages and disadvantages. The ILLIAC was designed in the mid 1960's for scientific calculations. The MPP was designed in the mid 1970's for LANDSAT image processing. Each of its 16,384 processors is only one bit wide. It has no built in fixed- or floating-point arithmetic--only a full adder.

Satellite image data are organized as arrays of picture elements (pixels). A typical image is a set of eight 3000x3000 arrays of 7-bit pixels. Each of the eight arrays represents the data recorded by one band (wavelength) of a sensor. Working with these data, the MPP can achieve a peak rate of nearly 7 billion additions per second. It can perform image correlation thousands of times faster than NASA's general purpose computers.

ARCHITECTURE

The MPP is a 128x128 array of processor elements which all operate together in lockstep. A central control unit distributes an instruction stream simultaneously to all PEs. Each processor operates on 1-bit data and addresses 1024 bits of parity checked random access memory. The elements of the MPP are (Figure 9.1):

1. The 128x128 processor array;

2. The array control unit;

3. The program and data management unit (PDMU);

4. The input/output interface; and

5. The staging buffer.

The MPP is a descendant of the ILLIAC IV: each processor is connected to its four nearest neighbors, and the entire array operates in lockstep under the direction of a single control unit.

Operating with a cycle time of 100 nanoseconds, the 16384 processor elements can perform $6.5 \cdot 10^9$ 8-bit integer additions per second or $1.8 \cdot 10^9$ 8-bit integer multiplications per second. Problems utilizing floating-point arithmetic were not originally envisioned for the MPP. NASA's design and specification were based upon use of the MPP on image processing applications. Nevertheless, the MPP can perform $4.3 \cdot 10^8$ additions per second or $2.1 \cdot 10^8$ multiplications per second in the 32-bit floating-point arithmetic format of the IBM 360.

The *staging buffer* was provided to transform satellite image data from standard telemetry form (serial by pixel) to a form amenable for parallel processing (serial by bit-plane).

Array Unit

Although the MPP appears to the programmer as a 128x128 processor array, it is actually an array of 128x132 processor elements. The additional 4-column group provides redundancy in the case of failure. Eight processor elements are contained in one chip as a 2x4 array. Two 1024x4-bit memory chips are associated with the 8 processor elements on a single chip.

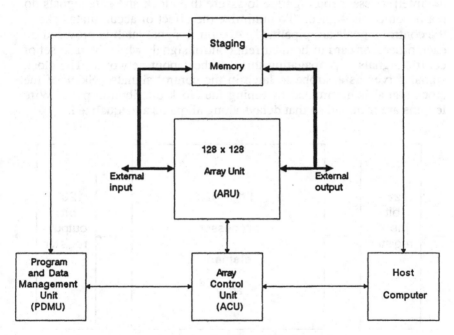

Figure 9.1 Massively parallel processor

Figure 9.2 illustrates the major components of the array unit (ARU):

1. The processor element array;

2. The 128-bit input and 128-bit output registers;

3. The fan-out module;

4. The corner point decode unit; and

5. The sum-or module.

All 16384 PEs execute the same instruction at one time. The 17 PE control lines, 10 memory address lines ($\log_2 1024$), memory control, and system clock must all be distributed to each PE without significant skew. The skew must be maintained to tolerances less than the interprocessor routing time to assure that clock and data signals do not become misaligned. To minimize the effect of accumulated skew, the control signals are pipelined. A control-signal latch is provided on each processor card to hold current control signals while the next set of control signals is propagating through the fanout network. The clock signal serves as a strobe to latch in the control signals. Skew of the clock signal is minimized by tuning the clock distribution path. Wire lengths are trimmed so that delays along all paths are equalized.

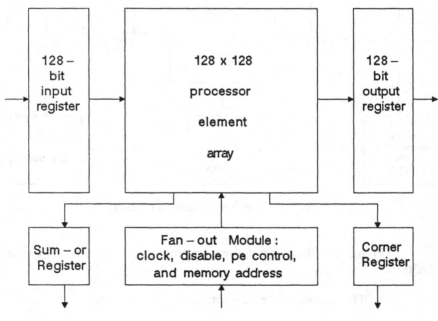

Figure 9.2 Array unit

Processor Element. The processor element (PE) provides logical and arithmetic capability on a 1-bit data path. Eight processor elements, each containing approximately 250 gates and 1000 transistors, are contained within a single processor element chip. The clock cycle is 100 nanoseconds. The major components of the processor element are:

1. Registers;

2. Full adder;

3. Shift register;

4. Logic unit; and

5. Random access memory.

The processor element is driven by a microprogram. Several of the control lines are decoded; the remainder have specific gating functions. This allows variations within an operation type, depending upon which registers are gated in as operands.

As was the case with the ILLIAC IV, MPP operations may be masked. When masking is specified (by a microprogram control line), an operation is performed by only those PEs where the mask register, G, is set. Operations involving the A, B, C, and P registers, as well as the shift register can be masked (Figure 9.3).

Registers. The MPP's 1-bit registers are latched and pipelined. If a register both provides input and receives output during a single operation, the original value will be used as input and, at the end of the cycle, will be replaced by any output developed.

The A register provides one operand to the full adder and receives the shift register output, the data bus, or zero under microprogram control.

The B register receives the full adder sum-output and provides input to the shift register or to the data bus.

The C register receives the full adder carry-output and provides carry-input to the full adder or to the data bus.

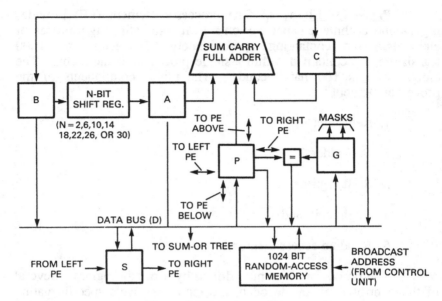

Figure 9.3 Processor element

The G register controls conditional operations of the PE, provides one operand to the equivalence/masked negate unit (which can provide the result to the data bus), and is loaded from the data bus.

The P register can provide an operand to the full adder, to the data bus, or to the equivalence/masked negate unit (which can provide the result to the data bus). The P register can also provide operands to, and receive operands from, the P registers of nearest neighbor processor elements. The P register receives the result bit of the logic unit.

The S register receives data from, or provides data to, the data bus. The S register participates in input/output operations by providing data to the PE to its right and receiving data from the PE to its left.

Full adder. The full adder receives a 1-bit input from each of the A and P registers and a carry input from the C register. The adder may be operated as a half adder if the P register is not gated in. The output of the full adder is a sum bit in the B register and a carry bit in the C register (for the next bit position). The C register is set or cleared during an instruction by one of the microprogram control lines.

Shift register. The shift register is located between the A and B registers of the adder. It consists of five elements: (a) 4-bit shift register segment, (b) 8-bit shift register segment, (c) 16-bit shift register segment, and (d) two latches. Routing of data through or around the 4-bit, 8-bit and 16-bit shift registers is controlled by microprogram control lines. By choosing to route data through the three shift register segments, the shift register may be made to appear to have a length of 2, 6, 10, 14, 18, 22, 26, or 30 stages. When working with the adder, where data are routed through the A and B registers as well, the shift register appears to have a length two stages greater than those given above. This allows the shift register, A register, and B register to conveniently manipulate 32-bit arithmetic data.

Logic unit.   Under microprogram control, the logic unit performs any of the sixteen boolean functions of two input variables. The P register and the data bus provide the inputs to the logic unit, and the P register receives the result.

Random access memory. Each PE may address 1024 bits of random access memory. As part of each instruction, a single memory address is provided to all of the PEs by the PE control unit.

Nearest Neighbor Routing. Each processor element P register is connected to its counterpart P register in the nearest neighbor PEs to the left, right, above, and below. During a routing operation, each PE reads the state of the P register in the selected nearest neighbor PE and stores the state in its own P register. The "nearest neighbor" may be as close as a PE on the same chip, or may be as far away as a PE on a different board. PEs at intermediate distances may be on different chips on the same board. Despite the wide variation in electrical distance between nearest neighbors (from millimeters of silicon for PEs on the same chip to .5 meter of wire for PEs on different boards), all PEs must route in a fixed time.

A topology register controls the nature of routing at the edges of the array. There are several different modes of edge routing which may be selected (Figure 9.4). Changes in the array topology configuration are expected to be infrequent. The hardware for effecting changes is straightforward and not highly optimized for speed.

In the simplest case, all four array edges are open. Zeros are supplied to replace data shifted into the array from an edge. Data shifted past an edge are lost.

a) THE 128 × 128 ARRAY; THE PROCESSOR AT X IS CONNECTED TO ITS NEAREST NEIGHBORS HORIZONTALLY AND VERTICALLY.

b) IN THIS CONFIGURAITON THE ARRAY ACTS AS A CYLINDER.

c) THE CONFIGURATION IS A 16384 ELEMENT VECTOR.

d) THIS CONFIGURATION IS A 16384 ELEMENT CYCLE.

Figure 9.4 Interconnection topologies

The array may also be configured as a toroid. PEs in a row or column at the array edge (those with at least one coordinate which is 0 or 127) are connected with the corresponding PE of the opposite edge.

Left and right edges may be connected as a raster. In this mode, the rightmost PE of a row is connected to the leftmost PE of the row below. If the raster is closed, $PE_{127,127}$ is connected to $PE_{0,0}$. If the raster is open, $PE_{127,127}$ and $PE_{0,0}$ are not connected.

Rasters are not available involving the north and south edges because of complications arising from the need to skip over the 4-column group of PEs provided for redundancy.

Sum-OR. The MPP can simultaneously test all the PEs for zero. Previously, Goodyear implemented this on the STARAN as the Sum-OR. The Sum-ORs for the eight PEs on each chip are generated and combined, yielding the Sum-OR for each board. The board level signals are then combined to yield the Sum-OR for the entire array. The redundant 4-column group of PEs forces a zero Sum-OR into the OR tree.

Additional hardware is incorporated to simplify the problem of determining the location of a stuck-at-one failure in the Sum-OR tree. The tree is made up of signals collected by column. A priority encoder indicates the address of the first (lowest numbered) row presenting a one within a column. Diagnostic software, utilizing the column-disable capability, isolates the stuck-at-one fault.

Corner Bits. The corner bits operation returns a 16-bit word--the corners of the 16 squares resulting from dividing each axis into four segments. Since the redundant 4-column group may be disabled at any point within the array, another set of 16 PEs, offset by 4 columns, may return (shadow) corner bits. The appropriate corner bits are selected based on the position of the disabled 4-column group (Figure 9.5). For columns to the left of the disabled columns, the original corner bits are chosen . For columns to the right of the disabled columns, the shadow corner bits are chosen.

Input/Output. Input/output (I/O) is accomplished with the PE S register. The S register of each PE is connected to its nearest neighbors on the left and right. The S registers form 128 rows of shift registers, each 128 bits long (132 PEs are connected but four are disabled). The issues of clocking and skew, discussed earlier in connection with the PE nearest neighbor routing, must also be dealt with here.

An input operation reads a 128-bit column of data at the array's left edge. An output operation writes a 128-bit column of data at the array's right edge. In 128 cycles, an entire plane of data (128x128 bits) can be simultaneously written and read.

A pair of 128-bit latches is provided, one for input and one for output. Under control of the program and data management unit, the latches are connected either to external interfaces or to the staging buffer. The external interfaces allow data to be read to, and written from, devices separate from the MPP. The staging buffer provides a secondary semiconductor memory to hold intermediate results or to *corner turn* data.

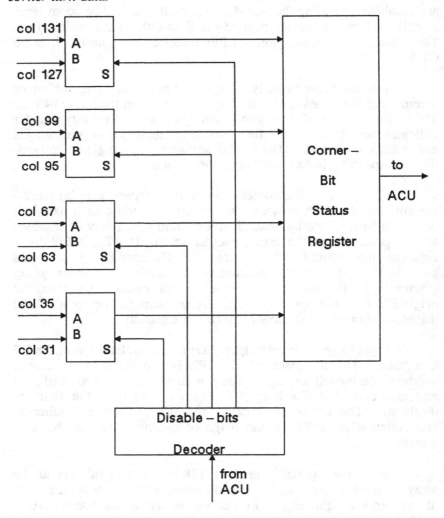

Figure 9.5 Corner bit selection

Memory. The MPP has a semiconductor memory of 1024 bits per PE. Two 45 nanosecond 1024x4-bit memory chips are used with each processor chip (8 PEs). The high speed required for memory was not attainable within the CMOS processor chip.

Memory error detection was not a high priority in the requirements and specifications for the MPP. Parity is provided, although its use requires the clock to run at 120 nanoseconds (instead of the usual 100 nanosecond cycle time). It should be noted, too, that the parity error indication is not available until three instructions after the failing memory reference occurs. Parity can not be checked during Sum-OR operations, as both functions share the fan-in logic.

Each 8-PE processor chip contains a parity generator. When data are stored, a parity bit is generated and stored in a separate parity memory. When data are fetched, the stored parity bit is fetched and compared with a parity bit generated from the data. If they do not agree, the parity-failure latch is set. After each memory fetch, the parity-failure latch is placed on the Sum-OR tree. Three instructions later, the array-wide parity-failure indicator is available for testing. Memory chips causing parity failures may be located by using the same techniques as those employed for Sum-OR failures.

Processor Element Instructions

Processor element instructions are selected by 17 control signals broadcast by the PE control unit. The 17 control signals are comprised of 5 fields: three 4-bit fields, a 2-bit field, and a 3-bit field. Each field controls an independent set of gates within the PE.

Control signal bits 0-3 determine:

1. Data bus source. The data bus source is selected from (a) memory, (b) the C register, (c) the B register, (d) the S register, (e) the P register, or (f) the value (P .eq. G).

2. P register logic. Control signal bits 4-7 select the boolean function applied to the data bus and P register. Any of the 16 possible boolean functions of two binary variable may be selected.

3. Shift register length. Control signal bits 4-7 select the apparent length of the shift register.

4. Adder. Control signal bits 8-11 select whether the C register is set or reset, or whether the B and C registers will receive the result of a full add or half add operation. If bit 8 is set, the G register is loaded from the data bus. If bits 9 and 11 are set, the Sum-OR tree is fed from the data bus.

5. P register routing. Control signal bits 4-7 select the direction (North, South, East, or West) from which the P register is loaded.

Control signal bit 2 enables masked operation of the PEs for P register logic and for P register routing.

Control signal bits 12-13 determine the source of data for the A register: (a) shift register, (b) data bus, or (c) clear a.

Control signal bit 14 causes a shift operation to occur.

Control signal bit 15 enables masked operation of the PEs for adder, shift register, or A register operations.

Control signal bit 16 writes the data bus into memory.

Array Control Unit

The array control unit (ACU) is responsible for running the application program. Within the ACU, the main control unit executes scalar arithmetic and other instructions not appropriate to the ARU. The main control unit calls upon the PE control unit to supply the ARU with control signals for the execution of array operations. The main control unit also calls upon the I/O control unit to execute input/output operations for the array. Each of the three control units operates concurrently (Figure 9.6):

1. The main control unit;

2. The PE control unit; and

3. The I/O control unit.

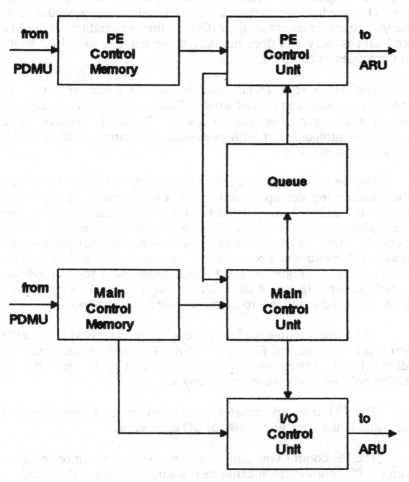

Figure 9.6 Array control unit

Main Control Unit

The main control unit (MCU) runs the application program. Scalar arithmetic, loop control, branching, and indexing are all performed within the MCU. When array operations are required, the

MCU queues a request for the PE control unit. After queueing a PE control unit request, the MCU continues operation without waiting. When I/O operations are required, the MCU calls the I/O control unit. If the I/O request is accepted, the MCU continues operation. If the I/O control unit is busy and does not accept the request, the MCU waits until the request is accepted.

The MCU is a 16-bit machine with a cycle time of 100 nanoseconds, containing 32,768 words of memory, 16 general purpose registers, and a supervisor-state register. It can be viewed as a conventional minicomputer with extensions for communicating to the PE and I/O control units.

Twelve scalar-return registers are included to receive the state of the common register upon return from a PE control unit call. The twelve 16-bit registers are organized as three 64-bit return values. The queue registers hold the values of parameters to be transferred to the PE control unit. Some of these parameters are: (a) address of operands, (b) number of operands, (c) operand length, and (d) stride. There are 13 queue registers: eight hold initial index register values, four hold scalar data for the common register, and one holds the entry address of the requested macro in the PE control unit memory.

The three group-disable registers allow the MCU to specify which 4-column group of PEs is disabled. This register may only be modified by an instruction in supervisor state and, generally, is modified only when diagnostic programs are run.

The I/O registers transfer parameters to, and from, the I/O control unit at the start, and finish, of I/O operations.

The PE control unit status register monitors a number of lines within the PE control unit, making their status available to the MCU.

PE Control Unit

The PE control unit (PECU) is responsible for generating control signals for the PEs and supplying them to the ARU. The PE control unit responds to array operation requests from the MCU. The major elements of the PE control unit (Figure 9.7) are:

1. Eight index registers;

2. A PECU memory;

3. A call queue;

4. A topology register;

5. An address generator;

6. A common register and selector;

7. A control-signal generator; and

8. A subroutine stack.

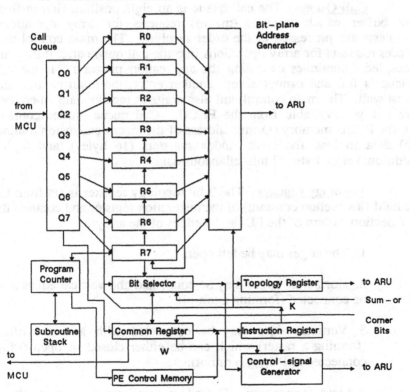

Figure 9.7 Processor element control unit

Index registers. The PECU contains a register file which provides eight 16-bit index registers. A single instruction can modify several index registers. The index registers are used to hold a loop counter. Register 0 can select a bit in the common-register. Registers 1-7 generate addresses for bit-plane memory accesses.

PECU Memory. The PECU memory holds the instructions for PECU macros which respond to calls placed in the call queue by the MCU. The result of executing a PECU macro is a control sequence for the ARU, causing the PEs to carry out an array operation. The PECU memory contains 8192 eight-byte instructions. It is loaded from the Program and Data Management Unit. Although a standard library of ARU operations is available, custom operations can be created and used when necessary.

Call Queue. The call queue is an eight position first-in-first-out buffer which receives (macro) requests for array operations. Requests are processed in the order received. The main control unit places requests for array operations into the call queue and, if they are accepted, continues executing the application program. If the call queue is full and cannot accept another entry, the main control unit must wait. The main control unit also waits to receive data when they are not yet available from the PECU. Call queue entries contain: (a) the PECU memory starting address of the macro expansion routine, (b) data to load the eight index registers (16 bytes), and (c) an additional eight bytes of miscellaneous data.

Topology register. The 3-bit topology register is set from the K field (instruction constant) of the instruction register and controls the connection pattern of the PEs at the edges of the array:

1. The edges may be left open.

2. Horizontal edges may be connected and vertical edges may be connected (forming a toroid).

3. Vertical edges may be connected with a 1-row offset (forming a raster) which can be either closed or open ($PE_{0,0}$ connected to $PE_{127,127}$ or not).

Address generator. The address generator combines the K field of the instruction register with an index register value to yield the bit-plane address for a load or store. The address is broadcast to all PE memories.

The index register specified must be in the range 1-7. If zero is specified, an index register does not participate in the generation of a storage address. The contents of the specified index register are added to the contents of the instruction constant, K, field. The sum is the bit-plane address.

Common Register and Selector. The 64-bit common register is used to hold global values which are broadcast to, or received from, the array. For example, a *scalar times matrix* operation maintains the scalar value in the common register. A *maximum* operation maintains the partial maxima in the common register during the search. The corner bits or an index register value may also be placed in the common register.

The common register selector addresses a single bit of the common register (under control of the instruction register K field). The selected bit is used to modify the PE control signals. The Sum-OR bit is gated into the common register selector, making it available to modify PE control signals.

Control-signal generator. The 17 control signals needed by each PE are broadcast by the control-signal generator. One line is the load/store flag for the array memory. The remaining 16 lines are derived from the instruction register. They are generated after the instruction register is modified by the common register and the common-register selector bit, W.

Subroutine Stack. The subroutine stack allows up to seven levels of subroutine nesting, holding the return address of each caller. Provision of the subroutine stack eliminates the need to use index registers for this purpose. Since the PECU macros are not generally available to the programmer, it was possible to employ a restricted subroutine access mechanism to gain speed.

I/O Control Unit. The I/O control unit is responsible for input/output between the array and either the staging buffer or external devices. A sequence of input/output commands specifies operation of the I/O control unit. The commands indicate: (a) source/sink of ARU data (external or staging buffer), (b) starting addresses for data blocks in the staging buffer, (c) number of columns in a bit-plane, and (d) whether more commands follow. There is one command for each bit plane to be transferred.

There is only one mode of input/output. The PE S registers are shifted to the right one column at a time. The column of S registers at the left edge receives a 128-bit column of input data from the input latch. The column of S registers at the right edge discharges a 128-bit column of output data to the output latch. If the staging buffer is selected, the I/O control unit buffer address registers indicate the locations to which output data are sent and from which input data are read. After each column is transferred, the buffer address registers are updated. Ordinarily, a bit-plane is comprised of 128 columns, although the bit-plane count register may be changed to a smaller value under program control. After an entire bit-plane has been transferred (i.e. the number of columns specified in the bit-plane count register has been transferred), the I/O control unit proceeds to the next I/O command.

Program and Data Management Unit

The Program and Data Management Unit (PDMU) is responsible for managing the MPP's external interface. It provides resources for job initiation, hardware and software diagnostics, program development, and management of databases and files. The PDMU is a conventional minicomputer, the DEC PDP11/34. The MCU memory, PECU memory, and the ARU I/O ports are mapped into the memory of the PDP11. This allows data transfers to occur under control of the PDMU.

Staging Buffer

The staging buffer is a mechanism for reformatting data as well as providing auxiliary memory. With a capacity of up to 64 megabytes and a maximum transfer rate to the ARU of 160 megabytes per second, the staging buffer allows the MPP to be used effectively for problems exceeding the array memory capacity.

The staging buffer is implemented as a main stager memory and two corner-turning units: one for input and one for output (Figure

9.8). The main stager memory can be configured with up to 32 banks, each with 256k 64-bit words. The full memory can transfer data to, or from, each corner-turning unit at a 160 megabyte per second rate. If the memory is not fully configured, the number of banks is reduced; data transfer rate is reduced proportionately; and word addresses must be an appropriate power of 2 (i.e. with 32 megabytes and 16 banks the main stager memory has an 80 megabyte per second transfer rate and word addresses are multiples of 2). Each word is stored with an additional 8 bit error correction field.

The corner turning units perform a coordinate transformation on data as they enter and leave the main stager memory. The input and output corner-turning units are symmetric. Each has 16k bytes of high speed (ECL) memory, arranged as 1024 x 128-bits. The corner-turning units transfer an entire column of data (128 bits) at one time. The input corner-turning unit receives data from either the external source or the ARU and transforms them into a main stager format. The output corner-turning unit receives data from the main stager and transforms them into the format needed by the ARU or the external device.

The corner-turning units are termed multidimensional access: data may be accessed by permutations of the memory address parameters. The provision of separate units allows rearrangement of data to be performed on-the-fly and overlapped with ARU processing. While the corner-turning units are formatting input and output data, the ARU receives data from the main stager, computes, and sends data back to the main stager.

The corner-turning units can access all banks of the main stager memory in one cycle. The input corner-turning unit permutes the data stream and sends it to the main stager for scatter-store as a sequence of 64-bit words with an associated address for each bank. The output corner-turning unit selects and fetches the appropriate word from each bank, further permutes them, and builds an output stream of consecutive bits.

For example, satellite data are received in frame, line, and pixel order. That is, a frame is transmitted as a sequence of lines. Each line is transmitted as a sequence of pixels, each of which is 8 bits long. The ARU requires the data to be received as sub-frames, with each sub-frame requiring eight memory planes (1 pixel). In order to transform the original data to this format, the input staging buffer rearranges them so that 128 consecutive bits form a 1-bit slice of a sub-frame. Eight slices comprise a complete sub-frame.

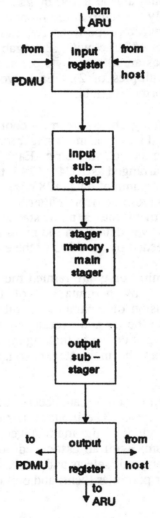

Figure 9.8 Staging buffer

The complete task of reformatting cannot be done at once since the input corner-turning memory holds only 16k bits. Instead, as data are received, they are partially reordered and stored in the main stager memory. The corresponding bits of successive pixels (every eighth bit) are put in sequence. These eight sequences (1-bit slices of sub-frames, 2048 bits, 128x16) are then scatter-stored into the main stager memory into their ultimate positions in the bit-plane data image being created.

The output corner-turning unit completes the task. It assembles eight 1-bit slices of sub-frames (2048 bits, 128x16) from the main stager memory into complete sub-frames (128x128) which are sent to the ARU. Although in this example the 1-bit slices are contiguous within the main stager memory, that will not be the case in general.

When computations performed by the ARU are completed the staging buffer reverses the input transformation by restoring the data to their original format and then returns them to the user.

Input data stream (pixels): $P_1, P_2, P_3, \ldots P_n$

Input data stream (bits): $P_{1,1}, P_{1,2}, \ldots P_{1,8}, P_{2,1}, \ldots P_{32768,8}$

Input corner-turning unit (16384 bits per input cycle).

$$P_{1,1}\, P_{1,2}\, P_{1,3}\ \ldots\ P_{1,8}\, P_{2,1}\ \ldots\ P_{2048,8}$$

$$P_{2049,1}\ \ldots\ P_{2049,8}\, P_{2050,1}\ \ldots\ P_{4096,8}$$

$$\vdots$$

$$P_{14337,1}\, P_{14337,2}\ \ldots\ P_{16384,7}\, P_{16384,8}$$

$$\vdots$$

$$P_{30721,1}\, P_{30721,2}\ \ldots\ P_{32768,7}\, P_{32768,8}$$

Main stager memory after 1 input cycle:

$$P_{1,1}\ P_{2,1}\ P_{3,1}\ ...\ P_{2048,1}\ 0\ ...\ 0$$

$$P_{1,2}\ P_{2,2}\ P_{3,2}\ ...\ P_{2048,2}\ 0\ ...\ 0$$

$$P_{1,3}\ P_{2,3}\ P_{3,3}\ ...\ P_{2048,3}\ 0\ ...\ 0$$

$$P_{1,4}\ P_{2,4}\ P_{3,4}\ ...\ P_{2048,4}\ 0\ ...\ 0$$

$$P_{1,5}\ P_{2,5}\ P_{3,5}\ ...\ P_{2048,5}\ 0\ ...\ 0$$

$$P_{1,6}\ P_{2,6}\ P_{3,6}\ ...\ P_{2048,6}\ 0\ ...\ 0$$

$$P_{1,7}\ P_{2,7}\ P_{3,7}\ ...\ P_{2048,7}\ 0\ ...\ 0$$

$$P_{1,8}\ P_{2,8}\ P_{3,8}\ ...\ P_{2048,8}\ 0\ ...\ 0$$

After 2 input cycles:

$$P_{1,1}\ P_{2,1}\ P_{3,1}\ ...\ P_{4096,1}\ 0\ ...\ 0$$

$$P_{1,2}\ P_{2,2}\ P_{3,2}\ ...\ P_{4096,2}\ 0\ ...\ 0$$

$$P_{1,3}\ P_{2,3}\ P_{3,3}\ ...\ P_{4096,3}\ 0\ ...\ 0$$

$$P_{1,4}\ P_{2,4}\ P_{3,4}\ ...\ P_{4096,4}\ 0\ ...\ 0$$

$$P_{1,5}\ P_{2,5}\ P_{3,5}\ ...\ P_{4096,5}\ 0\ ...\ 0$$

$$P_{1,6}\ P_{2,6}\ P_{3,6}\ ...\ P_{4096,6}\ 0\ ...\ 0$$

$$P_{1,7}\ P_{2,7}\ P_{3,7}\ ...\ P_{4096,7}\ 0\ ...\ 0$$

$$P_{1,8}\ P_{2,8}\ P_{3,8}\ ...\ P_{4096,8}\ 0\ ...\ 0$$

After 16 input cycles:

$$P_{1,1}\ P_{2,1}\ P_{3,1}\ \ \ldots\ \ P_{4096,1}\ \ \ldots\ \ P_{32768,1}$$

$$P_{1,2}\ P_{2,2}\ P_{3,2}\ \ \ldots\ \ P_{4096,2}\ \ \ldots\ \ P_{32768,2}$$

$$P_{1,3}\ P_{2,3}\ P_{3,3}\ \ \ldots\ \ P_{4096,3}\ \ \ldots\ \ P_{32768,3}$$

$$P_{1,4}\ P_{2,4}\ P_{3,4}\ \ \ldots\ \ P_{4096,4}\ \ \ldots\ \ P_{32768,4}$$

$$P_{1,5}\ P_{2,5}\ P_{3,5}\ \ \ldots\ \ P_{4096,5}\ \ \ldots\ \ P_{32768,5}$$

$$P_{1,6}\ P_{2,6}\ P_{3,6}\ \ \ldots\ \ P_{4096,6}\ \ \ldots\ \ P_{32768,6}$$

$$P_{1,7}\ P_{2,7}\ P_{3,7}\ \ \ldots\ \ P_{4096,7}\ \ \ldots\ \ P_{32768,7}$$

$$P_{1,8}\ P_{2,8}\ P_{3,8}\ \ \ldots\ \ P_{4096,8}\ \ \ldots\ \ P_{32768,8}$$

Output corner turning unit (16384 bits per output cycle):

$$P_{1,1}\ P_{2,1}\ P_{3,1}\ \ \ldots\ \ P_{2047,1}\ P_{2048,1}$$

$$P_{1,2}\ P_{2,2}\ P_{3,2}\ \ \ldots\ \ P_{2047,2}\ P_{2048,2}$$

$$P_{1,3}\ P_{2,3}\ P_{3,3}\ \ \ldots\ \ P_{2047,3}\ P_{2048,3}$$

$$P_{1,4}\ P_{2,4}\ P_{3,4}\ \ \ldots\ \ P_{2047,4}\ P_{2048,4}$$

$$P_{1,5}\ P_{2,5}\ P_{3,5}\ \ \ldots\ \ P_{2047,5}\ P_{2048,5}$$

$$P_{1,6}\ P_{2,6}\ P_{3,6}\ \ \ldots\ \ P_{2047,6}\ P_{2048,6}$$

$$P_{1,7}\ P_{2,7}\ P_{3,7}\ \ \ldots\ \ P_{2047,7}\ P_{2048,7}$$

$$P_{1,8}\ P_{2,8}\ P_{3,8}\ \ \ldots\ \ P_{2047,8}\ P_{2048,8}$$

$$\vdots$$

$$P_{2049,8}\ P_{2050,8}\ \ \ldots\ \ P_{4095,8}\ P_{4096,8}$$

REFERENCES AND BIBLIOGRAPHY

[All64] Allard, R. W., Wolf, K. A., Zemlin, R. A., "Some Effects of the 6600 Computer on Language Structures," *Communications of the ACM*, 7, No. 2, February 1964.

[AMD64] Amdahl, G. M., Blaauw, G. A., Brooks, F. P. Jr., "Architecture of the IBM System/360," *IBM Journal of Research and Development*, **8**, No. 2, 87-101, April 1964.

[AMD64] Amdahl, G. M., Blaauw, G. A., Brooks, F. P. Jr., Padegs, A., Stevens, W. Y., "The Structure of System/360," *IBM Systems Journal*, 3, Nos . 2&3, 119-261, 1964.

[AMD67] Amdahl, G. M., "Validity of the single processor approach to achieving large scale computing capabilities," *Proceedings 1967 Spring Joint Computer Conference,* 483-485, AFIPS Press, Chicago, 1967.

[AND67] Anderson, D.W., Sparacio, F. J., Tomasulo, R. M., "Machine Philosophy and Instruction Handling," *IBM Journal of Research and Development*, **11**, No. 1, 8-24, January 1967.

[AND67a] Anderson, S. F., Earle, J. G., Goldschmidt, R. E., Powers, D. M., "Floating-Point Execution Unit," *IBM Journal of Research and Development*, **11**, No. 1, 34-53, January 1967.

[BAR68] Barnes, G. H., Brown, R. M., Kato, M., Kuck, D. J., Slotnick, D. L., Stokes, R. A., "The ILLIAC IV Computer," *IEEE Transactions on Computers*, **C-17**, No. 8, August 1968.

[BAS77] Baskett, F., Keller, T. W., "An Evaluation of the Cray-1 Computer," *High Speed Computer and Algorithm Organization*, Kuck, D., et al., editors, 71-84, Academic Press, New York, 1977

[BAT68] Batcher, K. E., "Sorting Networks and Their Applications," *Proceedings, Spring Joint Computer Conference*, Thompson Book Co., Washington, 307-314, 1968

[BAT73] Batcher, K. E., "STARAN/RADCAP Hardware Architecture," *Proceedings, 1973 Sagamore Conference on Parallel Processing*, IEEE Press, New York, 147-152 1973.

[BAT76] Batcher, K. E., "The Flip Network in STARAN," *Proceedings of the 1976 International Conference on Parallel Processing*, IEEE Computer Society Press, Long Beach, 1976.

[BAT77] Batcher, K. E., "The Multidimensional Access Memory in STARAN," *IEEE Transactions on Computers*, **C-26**, No.2, 174-177, February 1977.

[BAT80] Batcher, K. E., "Design of a Massively Parallel Processor," *IEEE Transactions on Computers*,**C-29**, No. 9, 836-840, September 1980.

[BAT82] Batcher, K. E., "Bit-Serial Parallel Processing Systems, *IEEE Transactions on Computers*, **C-31**, No. 5, 363-376, May 1982.

[BAT83] Batcher, K. E., *MPP PE Control Unit*, Goodyear Aerospace Corporation, Akron, 1983.

[BLO59] Bloch, E., "The Engineering Design of the Stretch Computer," *Proceedings of the Eastern Joint Computer Conference*, Spartan Press, 48-58, 1959.

[BLO60] Blosk, R. T., "The Instruction Unit of the Stretch Computer," *Proceedings of the Eastern Joint Computer Conference*, 18, 299-324, December 1960.

[BOL67] Boland, L. J., Granito, G. D., Marcotte, A. U., Messina, B. U., Smith, J. W., "Storage System," *IBM Journal of Research and Development*, 11, No. 1, 54-68, January 1967.

[BOU72] Bouknight, W. J., Denenberg, S. A., McIntyre, D. E., Randall, J. M., Sameh, A. H., Slotnick, D. L., "The ILLIAC IV System," *Proceedings of the IEEE*, 60, No. 4, April 1972.

[BUC62] Bucholtz, W., editor, *Planning a Computer System*, McGraw-Hill Publishing Co., New York, 1962.

[BUR70] Burnett, G., Coffman, E. Jr., "A Study of Interleaved Memory Systems," *Proceedings 1970 Spring Joint Computer Conference*, 464-474, AFIPS Press, Chicago, 1970.

[BUR72] Burroughs Corporation, *ILLIAC IV Systems Characteristics and Programming Manual*, Paoli, 1972.

[CHE64] Chen,T. C., "The Overlap Design of the IBM System/360 Model 92 Central Processing Unit," *Proceedings 1964 Fall Joint Computer Conference*, Part II, 73-80, 1964.

[CHE71] Chen, T. C., "Parallelism, Pipeling, and Computer Efficiency," *Computer Design*, 69-74, January 1971.

[CHE75] Chen, T. C., "Overlap and Pipeline Processing," *Introduction to Computer Architecture*, H. S. Stone, (Ed.), Science Research Associates, Chicago, 1975

[CHU62] Chu, Y., *Digital Computer Design Fundamentals*, McGraw-Hill Publishing Company, New York, 1962.

[COC59] Cocke, J., Kolsky, H. G., "The Virtual Memory in the Stretch Computer," *Proceedings of the Eastern Joint Computer Conference*, 16, 82-93, December 1959.

[CON70] Control Data Corporation, *Control Data STAR-100 Computer*, St. Paul, 1970.

[CON80] Control Data Corporation, *CDC CYBER 200 Model 205 Computer System*, Minneapolis, 1980.

[CRA76] Cray Research, Inc., *Cray-1 Computer System*, Bloomington, 1976.

[CRA78] Cray, S. R. Jr., "Computer Vector Register Processing," *United States Patent*, No. 4,128,880, 1978.

[DAV69] Davis, R. L., "The ILLIAC IV Processing Element," *IEEE Transactions on Computers*, **C-18**, No. 9, September 1969.

[ELR70] Elrod, T. H., "The CDC 7600 and Scope 76," *Datamation*, **16**, No. 4, 80-85, April 1970.

[EVA86] Evans, B. O., "System/360: A Retrospective View," *Annals of the History of Computing*, AFIPS Press, Chicago, 1986.

[FEI83] Feilmeier, M., Joubert, G. R., Schendel, U., editors, *Parallel Computing 83*, Elsevier Science Publishers, Amsterdam, 1983.

[FLO63] Flores, I., *The Logic of Computer Arithmetic*, Prentice-Hall, Englewood Cliffs, 1963.

[FLY72] Flynn, M., "Some Computer Organizations and Their Effectiveness," *IEEE Transactions on Computers*, **C-21**, No. 9, 948-960, September 1972.

[FRE61] Freiman, C. V., "Statistical Analysis of Certain Binary Division Techniques," *Proceedings of the IRE*, **49**, No. 1, 91-103, January 1961.

[GRA70] Graham, R., "The Parallel and the Pipeline Computers," *Datamation*, **16**, No. 4, 68-71, April 1970.

[GRE63] Gregory, J., McReynolds, R., "The SOLOMON Computer,"*IEEE Transactions on Electronic Computers*, **EC-12**, No. 12, 774-81, December 1963.

[HAM50] Hamming, R. W., "Error Detection and Correcting Codes," *Bell System Technical Journal*, **29**, No. 2, 147-160, April 1950.

[HOB70] Hobbs, L. C., editor, *Parallel Processor Systems, Technologies and Applications*, Spartan Books, New York, 1970.

[HOC81] Hockney, R. W., Jesshope, C. R., *Parallel Computers*, Adam Hilger Ltd, Bristol, 1981.

[HOC84] Hockney, R. W., "Peformance of Parallel Computers," *High-Speed Computation*, 159-175Kowalik, J. S., (editor), Springer-Verlag, Berlin, 1984

[IVE62] Iverson, K. E., *A Programming Language*, Wiley, New York, 1962.

[JOR84] Jordan, H. F., "Experience with Pipelined Multiple Instruction Streams," *Proceedings of the IEEE*, 72, No. 1, 113-123, January 1984.

[KEL75] Keller, R. M., "Look-Ahead Processors," *Computing Surveys*, 7, No. 4, 177-195, December 1975.

[KNU70] Knuth, D. E., "An Empirical Study of FORTRAN Programs," Stanford University, Report CS-186, 1970

[KOG81] Kogge, P. M., *The Architecture of Pipelined Computers*, McGraw Hill Publishing Company, New York, 1981.

[KOW85] Kowalik, J. S., editor, *Parallel MIMD Computation: HEP Supercomputer and its Applications*, MIT Press, Cambridge, 1985.

[LED60] Ledley, R. S., *Digital Computer and Control Engineering*, McGraw-Hill Book Company, New York, 1960.

[LIN82] Lincoln, N. R., "Technology and Design Tradeoffs in the Creation of a Modern Supercomputer," *IEEE Transactions on Computers*, C-31, No. 5, 349-362, May 1982.

[LOR72] Lorin, H. *Parallelism in Hardware and Software*, Prentice-Hall, Englewood Cliffs, 1972.

[MAC61] MacSorley, O. L., "High-Speed Arithmetic in Binary Computers," *Proceedings of the IRE*, 49, 67-91, January 1961.

[MCI70] McIntyre, E., "An Introduction to the ILLIAC IV Computer," *Datamation*, **16**, No. 4, 60-67, April 1970.

[MUR70] Murphey, J. O., Wade, R. M., "The IBM 360/195 in a World of Mixed Jobstreams," *Datamation*, **16**, No. 4, 72-79, April 1970.

[RAM77] Ramamoorthy, C. V., Li, H. F., "Pipeline Architecture," *Computing Surveys*, **9**, No. 1, 61-102, March 1977.

[RAU77] Rau, B. R., Rossman, G. E., "The Effect of Instruction Fetch Strategies upon the Performance of Pipelined Instruction Units," *The 4th Annual Symposium on Computer Architecture, Conference Proceedings*, 80-89, IEEE, 1977

[RIG84] Riganati, J. P., Schneck, P. B., "Supercomputing," *Computer*,**17**, No. 10, 97-113 October 1984

[ROB58] Robertson, J. E., "A New Class of Digital Division Methods," *IRE Transactions on Electronic Computers*, **EC-7**, No. 3, 218-22, September 1958.

[RUS78] Russell, R. M., "The Cray-1 Computer System," *Communications of the ACM*, **21**, No. 1, 63-72, January 1978.

[SLO62] Slotnick, D. L., Borck, W. C., McReynolds, R. C., "The SOLOMON Computer," *AFIPS Conference Proceedings*, AFIPS Press, 97-107

[SLO67] Slotnick, D. L., "Unconventional Systems," *Proceedings 1967 Spring Joint Computer Conference*, 477-481, AFIPS Press, Chicago, 1967.

[SLO71] Slotnick, D. L., "The Fastest Computer," *Scientific American*, **224**, No. 2, 76-87, February 1971.

[SLO82] Slotnick, D. L., "The Conception and Development of Parallel Processors--A Personal Memoir," *Annals of the History of Computing*, **4**, No. 1, 20-30, January 1982.

[SMI78] Smith, B. J., "A Pipelined, Shared Resource MIMD Computer," *Proceedings of the 1978 International Conference on Parallel Processing*, 6-8, IEEE, 1978

[STO80] Stone, H. S. (editor), *Introduction to Computer Architecture*, Science Research Associates, New York, 1980

[THO64] Thornton, J. E., "Parallel Operation in the Control Data 6600," *AFIPS Conference Proceedings*, AFIPS Press, 33-40, 1964.

[THO70] Thornton, J. E., *Design of a Computer: The Control Data 6600*, Scott, Foresman and Company, Glenview, 1970.

[THU75] Thurber, K. J., Wald, L. D., Associative and Parallel Processors," *Computing Surveys*, 7, No. 4, 215-255, December 1975.

[TOM67] Tomasulo, R. M., "An Efficient Algorithm for Exploiting Multiple Arithmetic Units," *IBM Journal of Research and Development*, 11, No. 1, 25-33, January 1967.

[WAL64] Wallace, C. S., "A Suggestion for a Fast Multiplier," *IEEE Transactions on Computers*, EC-13, 14-17, January 1964.

[WAT72] Watson, W. J., "The TIASC -- A Highly Modular and Flexible Supercomputer Architecture," *Fall Joint Computer Conference*, AFIPS Press, Montvale, 221-228, 1972

INDEX

Accept stack 94, 95
Adder 83, 125, 128, 162
   carry-lookahead 85
   carry-propagate 32, 89, 128, 129
   carry-save 88, 128
Advanced station 120, 122, 124
Barrel switch 127
Busy bit 76-78, 82
Carry-lookahead adder 85
Carry-propagate adder 32, 89, 128, 129
Carry-save adder 88, 128
CDC 6600 69, 100, 135, 136
CDC 7600 135, 136
Chaining 140, 150, 151
Combining 26, 96
Common data bus 76, 80, 150
Conditional mode 65, 66, 72, 75
Conflict
   direct 49
      result register 50
   function unit 149
   indirect 50

   memory 64
   operand register 149
   output operand 160
   register file write 160
   source operand 160
Cray-2 135
Cray-XMP 135
Divider 62, 162
Final station 120, 122, 124
Final station queue 121
Floating-point buffer 74, 81, 156
Forwarding 26, 96, 150
Function unit 38, 47, 48, 49, 50, 51, 75, 81, 82, 100, 136, 139, 149
IBM 30xx 59
IBM 360 9, 21, 54, 62, 89
   model 91 26, 100, 135, 147, 150, 156, 157
IBM 370 59
IBM 704 21
IBM 7090 37, 43, 61, 100
Immediate 14, 58, 110
Imprecise interrupt 68
Instruction buffer 64, 66, 77, 80, 147, 148
Instruction control unit 23
Instruction issue 49, 69, 77, 136, 149, 151, 156, 159, 160
Instruction look-ahead 25, 122
Instruction stack 48, 63, 105, 107, 159
Instruction unit 63
Interleave 36, 42, 43
Latency 25, 62, 138, 150, 155
Loop mode 66, 80
Magnetic core 8, 24, 43, 102
Multiplier 32, 86, 128, 162
Parallel arithmetic unit 32
Pipeline 23, 62, 83, 86, 100, 108, 109, 136, 139, 141, 150, 155, 157,
      160, 161
Priority unit 158
Processing element 120, 124, 125, 130
Request stack 94, 95, 97
Reservation 51, 78, 81, 82, 83, 148, 149
Result-address registers 160
Scalar 120, 136, 144, 155, 156, 157, 159
Scoreboard 48

Serial arithmetic unit 29
Shortstop 108, 157
STAR-100 155, 159, 160
Storage data buffer 95
Store address register 94, 95
Store data buffer 74, 94, 156
Stretch 7, 53
Superword 102, 157, 158
Thin-film 54, 93
Variable field length 13, 70, 72
Variable-length byte strings 101, 107
Vector 100, 102, 105, 108, 109, 110, 112, 117, 136, 138, 139, 141,
        145, 149, 150, 151, 155, 159

Printed in the United States
By Bookmasters